SIR, WE WOULD LIKE TO SEE JESUS

SIR,
WE WOULD LIKE
TO SEE JESUS

Homilies from a Hilltop

WALTER J. BURGHARDT, S.J.
Theologian in Residence
Georgetown University

PAULIST PRESS
New York/Ramsey

The Publisher gratefully acknowledges use of excerpts from *The Little Prince* by Antoine de Saint Exupéry; copyright 1943, 1971 by Harcourt Brace Jovanovich, Inc. Reprinted and reproduced by permission of the publisher.

Drawings by Silvia Termes.
Cover design by Tim McKeen.

Library of Congress
Catalog Card Number: 82-60589

ISBN: 0-8091-0338-9

Published by Paulist Press
545 Island Road, Ramsey, N.J. 07446

Printed and bound in the
United States of America

TABLE OF CONTENTS

v

Handwritten annotations in margin: Excellent · Excellent · Excellent — Beatitudes · O.K. · Good

FEASTS

MEDLEY

EPILOGUE

"Now among those who went up
to worship at the feast
were some Greeks.

"So these came to philip
who was from Bethsaida in Galilee
and said to him:
'Sir, we would like to see Jesus.'"

(Jn 12:20-21)

PREFACE

The surprisingly warm welcome accorded my last book of homilies, *Tell the Next Generation* (Paulist, 1980), has encouraged me to offer this fresh set to the Christian clergy and laity. These differ in several significant ways from the previous collection. First, all the homilies are of recent vintage: from May 1979 to December 1981. Second, all were preached within the context of the liturgy. Third, with only three exceptions the homilies were originally delivered in Dahlgren Chapel on the campus of Georgetown University (hence the subtitle *Homilies from a Hilltop*—not to be confused with the Sermon on the Mount).

Friends who have followed this pilgrim's progress should discover—if not in the homilies themselves, at least in the Prologue—the distance I've traveled in my approach to preaching. Most important, I suggest, is a shift in stress from the concept to the image, stemming from a growing realization that a homilist's primary function is not indoctrination but evocation. The homily at its best evokes a religious response.

I hope, above all, that readers will find between these covers some meaty spiritual reading—not so much material to be preached as stimulus for the spirit, a help for believing Christians to "see Jesus" not with my eyes but with their own.

Walter J. Burghardt, S.J.

PROLOGUE

Burghardt, Walter J., *Sir, We Would Like to See Jesus*, (NY: Paulist, 1982)

DOES MY DRAWING FRIGHTEN YOU?
Preaching as Imagining

Do you remember Saint-Exupéry's *Little Prince*? I'm thinking specifically of the opening pages:

> Once when I was six years old I saw a magnificent picture in a book, called *True Stories from Nature*, about the primeval forest. It was a picture of a boa constrictor in the act of swallowing an animal. Here is a copy of the drawing.

> In the book it said: "Boa constrictors swallow their prey whole, without chewing it. After that they are not able to move, and they sleep through the six months that they need for digestion."
>
> I pondered deeply, then, over the adventures of the jungle. And after some work with a colored pencil I succeeded in making my first drawing. My Drawing Number One. It looked like this:

> I showed my masterpiece to the grown-ups, and asked them whether the drawing frightened them.
>
> But they answered: "Frighten? Why should any one be frightened by a hat?"
>
> My drawing was not a picture of a hat. It was a picture of a

3

boa constrictor digesting an elephant. But since the grown-ups were not able to understand it, I made another drawing: I drew the inside of the boa constrictor, so that the grown-ups could see it clearly. They always need to have things explained. My Drawing Number Two looked like this:

The grown-ups' response, this time, was to advise me to lay aside my drawings of boa constrictors, whether from the inside or the outside, and devote myself instead to geography, history, arithmetic and grammar. That is why, at the age of six, I gave up what might have been a magnificent career as a painter. I had been disheartened by the failure of my Drawing Number One and my Drawing Number Two. Grown-ups never understand anything by themselves, and it is tiresome for children to be always and forever explaining things to them.

So then I chose another profession, and learned to pilot airplanes. I have flown a little over all parts of the world; and it is true that geography has been very useful to me. At a glance I can distinguish China from Arizona. If one gets lost in the night, such knowledge is valuable.

In the course of this life I have had a great many encounters with a great many people who have been concerned with matters of consequence. I have lived a great deal among grown-ups. I have seen them intimately, close at hand. And that hasn't much improved my opinion of them.

Whenever I met one of them who seemed to me at all clear-sighted, I tried the experiment of showing him my Drawing Number One, which I have always kept. I would try to find out, so, if this was a person of true understanding. But, whoever it was, he, or she, would always say:

"That is a hat."

Then I would never talk to that person about boa constrictors, or primeval forests, or stars. I would bring myself down to his level. I would talk to him about bridge, and golf, and politics, and neckties. And the grown-up would be greatly pleased to have met such a sensible man.[1]

In recent years I have argued that four problems prevent to-day's homily from being any better than yesterday's sermon: fear of Sacred Scripture, ignorance of contemporary theology, un-awareness of liturgical prayer, and lack of proper preparation.[2] The list has a lamentable lacuna. I have left out the most serious lack of all: imagination. Without imagination the preacher limps along on one leg. You may have memorized Mark and ransacked Rahner, you may be an expert in things liturgical and put onerous hours into your homily; but if your homily is only a masterpiece of Cartesian clarity, you are in deep trouble. If you are forever ex-plaining things to grownups, drawing recognizable Christian hats, you are hardly a homilist.

To make this outrageous thesis palatable, let me develop it in three stages. First, what are we talking about when we speak of imagination? Second, what has imagination to do with preaching? Third, if imagination is so awfully important, what ought we homi-lists to do about it?

I

First then, what is this creature we call imagination?[3] To begin with, what is imagination *not?* It is not the same thing as fantasy. Fantasy has come to mean the grotesque, the bizarre. That is fan-tastic which is unreal, irrational, wild, unrestrained. We speak of "pure fantasy": It has no connection with reality. It is imagination run wild, on the loose, unbridled, uncontained.[4]

What is it, then? Imagination is the capacity we have "to make the material an image of the immaterial or spiritual."[5] It is a cre-ative power. You find it in Rembrandt's self-portraits, in Beetho-ven's *Fifth Symphony,* in the odor of a new rose or the flavor of an old wine. You find it in storytellers like C. S. Lewis and Tolkien, in dramatists like Aeschylus and Shakespeare, in poets from Sappho to e. e. cummings.

Now, when I say "capacity," I do not mean a "faculty" like in-tellect or will. I mean rather a posture of our whole person towards our experience.[6] It is a way of seeing. It is, as with Castaneda, look-ing for the holes in the world or listening to the space between sounds. It is a breaking through the obvious, the surface, the su-perficial, to the reality beneath and beyond. It is the world of won-der and intuition, of amazement and delight, of festivity and play.

Is all this too imaginative to be clear? Then let me sketch, in clear and distinct ideas, some of the ways in which imagination—specifically, religious imagination—comes to expression.

1) A vision. I mean "the emergence either in dream, trance, or ecstasy, of a pattern of images, words, or dreamlike dramas which are experienced then, and upon later reflection, as having revelatory significance."[7] Examples? Isaiah's vision of the Lord in the temple (Isa 6); Ezekiel's "four living creatures" (Ezek 1); Moses and Elijah appearing to Jesus and the disciples on the Mount of Transfiguration (Mt 17:1–9); Joan of Arc's "voices"; Teresa of Avila's visions of Christ; St. Margaret Mary's vision of the Sacred Heart.

2) Ritual. The form of ritual is action—action that is public, dramatic, patterned. A group enacts the presence of the sacred and participates in that presence, usually through some combination of dance, chant, sacrifice, or sacrament.[8]

3) Story. I mean a narrative—that is, a constellation of images—that recounts incidents or events. As Sallie TeSelle puts it, "We all love a good story because of the basic narrative quality of human experience: in a sense *any* story is about ourselves, and a *good* story is good precisely because somehow it rings true to human life. . . . We recognize our pilgrimage from here to there in a good story."[9] For the religious imagination, three types of stories are particularly important: parable, allegory, and myth.

The parable is a developed simile, usually quite short, in which the narrative is at once fictitious and true to life; from it a moral or spiritual truth is extracted. In a specially forceful way we recognize our pilgrimage in the parables of Jesus: "The kingdom of heaven is like treasure hidden in a field" (Mt 13:34). "There was a man who had two sons" (Lk 15:11). "There was a rich man clothed in purple . . . [and] a poor man . . . full of sores" (Lk 16:19–20).

Allegories are developed metaphors prolonged into continuous narratives, in which a series of actions are symbolic of other actions, while the characters often are types or personifications. You remember Bunyan's *Pilgrim's Progress,* the dream allegory that tells of the journey of Christian and Christiana through "the wilderness of this world" to Sion; Spenser's *Faerie Queene,* that richly imaginative work of moral allegory; Lewis' *Chronicles of Narnia,* a milestone in theological allegory, high festivity in the kingdom of the imagination, the Christian quest in terms a child can understand.

The myth is basically verbal. "It is a narration which conveys the meaning of human existence in relation to its destiny or origin, or the destiny or origin of the social group, nature, or cosmos of which it is a part, as these are grounded and penetrated by the sacred."[10] And so we can speak legitimately of the Creation myth or the Christian myth. For myth is not opposed to fact or to fancy. Its raw material may be fact or it may be fancy, "but its purpose is not to add yet another facet to our squirrels' nest of facts stored against some winter of the mind, nor to create an entertaining fantasy to titillate aesthetic delight." It intends "to narrate the fundamental structure of human being in the world. By the concreteness of its imagery, the universality of its intention, its narrative or story form, the myth evokes the identification and participation of those for whom it functions as revelatory."[11]

4) Symbol. What symbol means is not easy to say; for even within theology it does not have a univocal sense. Let me define it, with Dulles, as "an externally perceived sign that works mysteriously on the human consciousness so as to suggest more than it can clearly describe or define."[12] Not every sign is a symbol. A mere indicator ("This Way to Windsor") or a conventional sign (a word) is not a symbol. "The symbol is a sign pregnant with a depth of meaning which is evoked rather than explicitly stated."[13] It might be an artifact: a totem, a crucifix, the brazen serpent. It might be a person or an event: Moses leading the Israelites out of Egypt, Jesus Christ crucified and risen. It might be words or writings: the Bhagavad Gita, the Old and New Testaments. It might be a story: parable, allegory, myth.

5) The fine arts. I mean painting and poetry, sculpture and architecture, music, dancing, and dramatic art. I mean da Vinci and John Donne, the *Pietà* and Chartres, Beethoven's *Missa Solemnis,* David whirling and skipping before the Ark of the Covenant, the mystery dramas of the Middle Ages. I mean films.

From all this two significant conclusions emerge. First, imagination is not at odds with knowledge; imagination is a form of cognition. In Whitehead's words, "Imagination is not to be divorced from the facts: it is a way of illuminating the facts."[14] True, it is not a process of reasoning; it is not abstract thought, conceptual analysis, rational demonstration, syllogistic proof. Notre Dame of Paris is not a thesis in theology; Lewis' famous trilogy does not demonstrate the origin of evil; Hopkins is not analyzing God's image in us when he sings that "Christ plays in ten thousand places,/ Lovely in limbs, and lovely in eyes not his/ [plays] To the Father through the features of men's faces."[15] And still, imaging and imagining is a work of our intellectual nature; through it our spirit reaches the true, the beautiful, and the good.

Second, the imagination does not so much teach as evoke; it calls something forth from me. And so it is often ambiguous; the image can be understood in different ways. Do you remember the reporters who asked Martha Graham, "What does your dance mean?" She replied: "Darlings, if I could tell you, I would not have danced it!" Something is lost when we move from imagining to thinking, from art to conceptual clarity. Not that imagination is arbitrary, that *Swan Lake* or the Infancy Narrative or *Hamlet* or the Transfiguration is whatever anyone wants to make of it, my gut feeling. Hostile to a valid imagination is "the cult of imagination for itself alone; vision, phantasy, ecstasy for their own sakes; creativity, spontaneity on their own, without roots, without tradition, without discipline."[16] Wilder is right: "Inebriation is no substitute for paideia."[17] And still it is true, the image is more open-ended than the concept, less confining, less imprisoning. The image evokes our own imagining.

II

My second question: What has imagination to do with preaching? Not much; just everything. The scholar of mythology Joseph Campbell did not think much of us clergy; he said we have no imagination. Part of the reason is our older education: Imagination was identified with "bad thoughts," and bad thoughts were sexual phantasms, and these we confessed. Moreover, as the Carmelite William McNamara has complained, all through school we were taught to abstract; we were not led to contemplation, to immediate communion with reality, to loving admiration, experiential awareness. We were not taught to simply "see."

To put the problem in vivid relief, let me contrast two theories of preaching. Recently I read the contention of a priest that we should scrap the Vatican II homily and get back to instructional sermons. The critical Catholic problem, he felt, is abysmal Catholic ignorance. Our people, particularly the young, do not know "the faith." A trinitarian God and an incarnate Son, original and actual sin, one true Church and seven real sacraments, created grace and Uncreated Grace, the Mass as sacrifice and the pope as vicar of Christ, mortal sin and the Ten Commandments, the immorality of birth control and abortion—this is what our faithful must be taught. Vatican II? Why, Catholics don't know Baltimore Catechism One! And especially these days, when elementary Catholic education is vanishing, there is only one viable way to teach: via the Sunday sermon. Give them the dogma, the doctrine, and give it with consummate clarity, with unquestioning certitude.

I cannot agree. I grant that many a Catholic is distressingly ignorant of God's revelation, does not know what God took flesh to tell us. Somehow, somewhere they should learn this. But not *ex professo* in a homily. The homily, like the liturgy of which it is part and parcel, should proclaim, re-present, make effectively present "God's wonderful works in the history of salvation"; "the mystery of Christ" should be "made present and active within us."[18] But this is not done by a laundry list of dogmas to be believed, doctrines to be accepted. It is done by imagination.

Why? Because indoctrination plays upon one faculty of the human person: the intellect's ability to grasp ideas, concepts, propositions. It pays little heed to an old scholastic axiom, "Nothing is present in the intellect that was not previously present in the senses." Our ideas are triggered by sense experience. On the whole, then, the more powerful the sense experience, the more powerfully an idea will take hold. If I want to sell you on Spaghetti Bolognese or Beef Burgundy, I don't hand you a recipe; I let you smell it, taste it, savor it. If I want you to "see" the Holocaust, I won't just say "six million were exterminated"; I'll let you see the gas ovens, the mountains of human bones. It is not enough to tell you the score of Handel's *Messiah;* you must drink it in with your ears. It is one thing to hear "I love you," quite another to experience love's touch.

My thesis? The homily is a fascinating wedding of all those ways in which imagination comes to expression: vision and ritual, symbol and story (parable, allegory, and myth), the fine arts. This is the homily at its best, the homily that makes God's wonderful works come alive, immerses in the mystery, evokes a religious response.

A response—there's the magic word! The homily might be different if the task of the liturgy were simply to *recall* God's saving works, simply to *remember* the mystery that is Christ. Then I might merely explain lucidly what it all means. But there is more. If the liturgy must make the mystery "present and active within us," a homily should be evocative. I mean, it should help the believer to open up to God speaking now. Not a cold assent to a proposition; rather, "What do you want from me, O Lord?" And the most effective approach to this is not ratiocination, not demonstration; it is imagination.

The evidence for imagination's incomparable power surrounds us. We keep saying "A picture is worth a thousand words." Americans spend billions each year on movies, theatre, concerts. Students study to stereo, skip lectures readily when Bruce Springsteen comes to town. Jesuits too read the comics before the front page, go wild over sports—poetry in motion. Our children's supreme educator, for good or ill, is TV. Even the commercials, that sell products from head to foot essential for human existence, sell us with the greatest array of imaginative talent since the creation story in Genesis 1 and John's vision on Patmos.

And we homilists (so our patient people complain) mount the pulpit or approach the podium with the imagination of a dead fish. "Today, my dear brethren, Holy Mother Church in her age-old wisdom urges us once again to fix our eyes on eternal verities, to scorn passing fancies and the temptations of this world, to recognize in this valley of tears that we have no lasting habitation, that our hearts have been made for God and will be restless until they rest in Him." It recalls what a reviewer once said of Msgr. Ronald Knox, English convert, satirist, master of style: "One can look in vain in his *Sermons* for such unctuous phrases as 'Holy Mother the Church,' which some preachers use as carelessly and frequently as sailors use obscenities to conceal their inability for sustained communication."[19] The same Knox was once twitted by a bishop for reading his sermons from a prepared text—twitted a bit too long. At last Knox said: "Ah yes, Your Grace, I recognize the validity of your observations. I sensed it one day when I was about to mount the pulpit with my manuscript in my hand and I heard a gentleman in the first pew whisper to his wife, 'My God, another bloody pastoral!' "

The homily is an instrument; God uses it to speak to the soul. *God* speaks. The external word is indeed mine; but if God is to speak, my word has to open the way, not close off all avenues save mine. Not, therefore, "When you go back to your kitchen, this is what you must do." Rather, so artistic a presentation of a message that different people hear from God what they need to hear. Like a great piece of music—Bach's church cantatas, full of symbolism, allusion, and word painting in the context of the Lutheran service—the homily will have different meanings for different listeners, will touch them not where I live but where they live, where God wants them to live.

Here imagination is indispensable. The image is more open-ended than the concept; the image evokes imagining. This is not indifferentism: From my homily you should not emerge with a unitarian God, an Arian Christ, abortion on demand. No; I presume, or insinuate, or proclaim the tradition. Remember Wilder: "Inebriation is no substitute for paideia." And still I am not so much exposing as evoking, not so much imposing on the ignorant a revealed truth with specific applications as drawing the already faithful into the mystery of Christ in such a way that *they* can apply it, can say yes to a living God speaking now. The priest, Urban Holmes insists, is "one who incites people to imagine."[20]

III

My third question: If imagination is so awfully important, what ought we homilists to do about it? When I first approached this point, I fumbled long and wearily with specifics; I wanted, you see, to give you concrete applications! Read storytelling theologian John Shea; tune in on the apocalyptic vision of the TV preachers; immerse yourself in Lewis and Tolkien; shift your language from the abstract to the concrete; remember that the verb carries the action; listen to the flowers.

I do not retract all that; those suggestions could be of help. But suddenly I realized that we have a more basic need. What Catholic homilists require is a conversion; we need fresh insight into our priesthood. I can best illustrate this from my own life. Here I wed three elements: the "I," the revelation, the people.

First, I who communicate. For the first half of my priestly life, I was the most objective of human beings. Objectivity had been rooted in me—by scholastic philosophy, by a theology that lived off magisterial affirmations, by spiritual masters who stressed reason and will, suspected emotion and experience, despite St. Ignatius' sense-saturated Spiritual Exercises. The subjective had illegitimate parents: Protestantism and Modernism. At the altar, then, and behind the confessional screen, in teaching and preaching, in lecturing and counseling, the I was submerged, that Christ alone might appear. I rarely said "I," that only the truth might transpire. Until one day in the early sixties, when I had given a remarkably lucid response to a young lady's religious question. She looked at me a moment, then said: "And what do *you* think?" It was a harrowing moment. I am not an ecclesiastical computer, spewing forth the data fed me. I too am a symbol, a sign that says more than my words can express. In the pulpit *I* may well be the most powerful image of all.

Second, the revelation we communicate. How was it initially communicated? In my more callow days we had no problem: Divine revelation consists of truths set forth in the Bible and in authoritative Church pronouncements. God has embodied His revelation in propositional language so that it can claim our unswerving assent. Now I do not deny that revelation can be mediated through true propositions. I simply point out that a fresh vision permeates our century, permeates me: Revelation is symbolic disclosure.[21] Revelation is always mediated through an experience in the world—specifically, through symbol. I have no room to argue this here; let me illustrate it by one example, a key theme in the New Testament: the kingdom of God.

> As Norman Perrin points out, the "kingdom of God" in the preaching of Jesus is not a clear concept or idea with a single, univocal significance. Rather, it is a symbol that "can represent or evoke a whole range or series of conceptions or ideas" and thus bring the hearer into the very reality borne by the preaching of Jesus. Perrin profusely illustrates the symbolic nature of this language as found in the proverbial sayings of Jesus, in the Lord's Prayer, and especially in the Gospel parables. The constant factor in these diverse materials, he maintains, is the symbol of the kingdom of God, which had for Jewish audiences the power to evoke the faith-experience of God's dramatic action on behalf of His people and to elicit an appropriate response. To seek to pin down some one definite meaning of the term "kingdom of God," according to Perrin, would be to overlook the polysemic character of symbolic communication.[22]

This does not mean that revelation cannot be translated into objective doctrinal statements. It means that our biblical symbols, from the theophanies of Sinai through the cross of Christ to the descent of the Spirit, are too rich to be imprisoned in any single conception. Moreover, the knowledge that symbols give is not cold, abstract information; it is "participatory knowledge." A symbol is an environment I inhabit, live in, the way I live in my body; I recognize myself within the universe of meaning and value it opens up to me.[23] And because revelation is this sort of truth, it can transform us, initiate us into a saving relationship with God; it can radically influence our commitments and our behavior; and it can give us insight into mysteries reason cannot fathom.

Third, the people with whom we communicate. Early on, I took for granted that they came to the liturgy to learn, that the sheep needed to be led. The assumption is clear in an address I gave two decades ago to the Catholic Homiletic Society on preaching dogma.[24] I do not disown the address, but it was one-sided: How do I preach the truth attractively? I hardly mentioned the people "out there." The responsibility, as far as I can reconstruct it, was to give ear to my clear message and be seduced by its beauty. Late in life I have begun to grasp why some pulpits confront the preacher graphically with the request of the Greeks to Philip: "Sir, we would like to see Jesus" (Jn 12:21). How simple a request . . . and how stunning! Here is our burden and our joy: to help believing Christians to see Jesus—not with our eyes but with their own.

Given fresh insight, a kind of conversion, on these three levels—a homilist more open and free, a revelation charged with symbols, a people wanting to see Jesus—you will inevitably preach imaginatively, prepare imaginatively. First, you will find yourself inescapably part and parcel of your homily. What you preach will strike sparks because *you* are aflame with it. The word you speak will say so much more than the dictionary definition because that word has taken flesh in you. You have been captured by a dream, enraptured by a vision; you have your own "voices"; the world of the senses excites you; like Teresa of Avila, you can be ravished by a rose. You will feel ceaselessly reborn, thank God each dawn with e. e. cummings "for most this amazing day . . . for everything which is natural which is infinite which is yes."[25]

Second, God's word will never again seem "stale, flat, and unprofitable." For you will have discovered, with the Benedictine liturgiologist Nathan Mitchell, that "every symbol deals with a new discovery and every symbol is an open-ended action, not a closed-off object. By engaging in symbols, by inhabiting their environment, [you will] discover new horizons for life, new values and motivation."[26] The biblical symbols will overwhelm you with their many-splendored possibilities, their refusal to be imprisoned in a formula, their openness to fresh imaginings. You may even start saying, not "The kingdom of heaven is . . . ," but "The kingdom of heaven is like. . . ."

Third, once you realize that your people want not catechesis or theology but only to see Jesus, you are forced to find ways to satisfy their thirst. Rome and Rahner are only a foundation. For all their objective importance, neither John Paul's encyclical *Redemptor hominis* nor the "supernatural existential" is calculated to turn the faithful on. And so, like it or not, you will learn to dream dreams and see visions, retell the parables of Jesus in a modern idiom. You will create your own world of Christian imaging, learn not only to pray but to play, look for the holes in the world, listen to the space between sounds.

The alternative is terrifying. Without imagination we homilists are no more than pied pipers, and just as dangerous as the original. Like the Piper of Hamelin, we dress in a suit of many colors, pipe our strange melody, and many of the children follow us. But where do they end up? Where the children of Hamelin ended up. Look again at Saint-Exupéry's Drawing Number One:

Doesn't it frighten you? You may answer: "Frighten? Why should anyone be frightened by a hat?" But my drawing is not the picture of a hat. It is a cave, a cave packed with children, a closed-up cave, a cave with no air, no exit, no freedom. Doesn't *that* frighten you?

1
DAWN: GETTING THROUGH THE NIGHT
First Sunday of Advent (A)

- *Isaiah 2:1–5*
- *Romans 13:11–14*
- *Matthew 24:37–44*

Advent can be confusing. What are we about in the liturgy—in this liturgy that is supposed to symbolize what goes on in the rest of our lives? The Lord has come, and yet we prepare for his coming. He is risen, and still we ready a crib for him. We rejoice that he lives within us, and we clothe ourselves in purple. Has "the day of the Lord" dawned or hasn't it? Is Advent make-believe? Are we pretending that the Lord Jesus has not yet come?

The fact is, Advent expresses in symbol and ritual three stages in the human journey, in the Christian journey. Christ has come; Christ will come again; and Christ is here now. We remember the first; we look to the second; we live the third. All three are part and parcel of our lives; so all three have to find expression in our liturgy. A word on each.

I

First, Advent is a remembering. We recapture what a whole people, a special people, a loved people lived for centuries. Isaiah speaks of a "people who walked in darkness, who dwelt in a land of deep darkness" (Isa 9:2). With Christian hindsight, we see this darkness as a period of anxious waiting for a dawn that was dreadfully long in coming, a night that was shaped of slavery and slaughter, hunger and thirst, fidelity and idolatry, a night that was God's

17

strange way of preparing His people for a new day, for the dawning of a light beyond their wildest imagining. Remember how the father of John the Baptist, "filled with the Holy Spirit" (Lk 1:67), prophesied to the eight-day-old infant:

And you, child, will be called the prophet of the Most High;
for you will go before the Lord to prepare His ways,
to give knowledge of salvation to His people
in the forgiveness of their sins,
through the tender mercy of our God,
when the day shall dawn upon us from on high
to give light to those who sit in darkness and in the shadow of
    death,
to guide our feet into the way of peace.

(Lk 1:76–79)

For centuries this world of sin had walked in darkness. The darkness was not pious poetry; it was total evil in conflict with God. It is the world of which the Psalmist sang:

The Lord looks down from heaven upon the children of men,
    to see if there are any that act wisely,
    that seek after God.
They have all gone astray, they are all alike corrupt;
    there is none that does good,
    no, not one.

(Ps 14:2–3)

Into this darkness the light shone one midnight clear, "the true light that enlightens every man" (Jn 1:9). That light was not some flickering flame; it was a person, the Son of God tented in human flesh. It is the Christ who said of himself, "I am the light of the world; he who follows me will not walk in darkness, but will have the light of life" (Jn 8:12). This was the light that was not eclipsed even on Calvary, when "there was darkness over the whole earth" (Lk 23:44). This was the light that rose at Easter dawn for our redemption.

This is what our liturgy remembers: centuries of darkness, lifted by a light unparalleled in history. We remember the human family groping in the gloom of ignorance and sin, yearning for "the day of the Lord" but unable to make it dawn. And we recall how the darkness was dissipated when the Light of the World shone in the world he had shaped. True, Jesus is no longer an infant, but he was; he no longer lies in a manger, but he did—and, literally, it made all the difference in the world. And so we remember it. He did come.

II

Second, Advent not only looks back, it looks ahead. We not only recall Christ's first coming, we anticipate his final coming. The trouble is, that end-time is wrapped in darkness. To begin with, we do not know *when* he will come. Some Christians, indeed, are sure they do know: The end is soon, it may be any moment now. College students in Virginia assured me recently with passionate conviction that the hour is here. In the Synoptic signs, in the predictions of Paul, in the Revelation to John they discovered this present generation. It's all here and now: the portents in sky and on earth, the four horsemen, the beast from the sea and the beast from the earth, the kings that make war on the Lamb, the harlot Babylon, the number 666. Even the Antichrist is here—though no longer Nero or Mohammed, and only possibly the pope.

No, my friends. We may be uncommonly clever at reading signs; but all our cleverness, I'm afraid, must break down before the words of Jesus: "You do not know on what day your Lord is coming" (Mt 24:42). St. Paul thought he knew, and Paul was wrong—wrong so far by nineteen centuries.

Nor do we know *how* Christ will come. The New Testament images and symbols are vivid enough: He will come "on the clouds of heaven with power and great glory" (Mt 24:30); "his angels will gather his elect from the four winds with a loud trumpet call" (v. 31); we shall rise from our graves "to meet the Lord in the air" (1 Thess 4:17). But the pictures and poetry of the first century tell us very little about the how. We know only that Christ will come again, that when he comes the power of evil will be swept utterly away, that then his kingdom will come in its eternal richness. Light indeed at the end of the tunnel—the glory of God; but right now the tunnel seems dreadfully dark.

The point is: When Scripture focuses on Christ's final coming, the stress is not on when and how. Interesting issues, of course, but not crucial. Two questions are crucial. First, whenever Christ comes, however he comes, will you be ready? Second, how are you readying Christ's return, how are you preparing God's kingdom?

III

Precisely there you have my third point. We not only look back on a first coming, forward to a final coming. We are not caught between a past that is gone and a future not yet here. What links yesterday and tomorrow is today. We are to live now a life that Christ's first coming made possible; and by living that life now, we prepare for his final coming. He is no longer in a crib of straw, not yet on clouds of glory. But he is here. The light shines in the darkness . . . now.

But does it really? Oh yes, Christ is here; my faith affirms it. We gather together in his name, and so he is here among us. We proclaim his word, and that word takes flesh, the flesh of the Word. I murmur "This is my body," and the altar quivers with his sacramental presence. But tell me honestly, do you actually find Christ lighting up the darkness in you, the darkness around you?

There is a darkness in all of us. We were born in darkness. Black may indeed be beautiful, but not the blackness that enveloped our birth. Over that birth hung a hateful inheritance: centuries of sin, eons of ignorance, an ageless legacy of what St. Paul called "the works of the flesh: immorality, impurity, licentiousness, idolatry, sorcery, enmity, strife, jealousy, anger, selfishness, dissension, party spirit, envy, murder, drunkenness, carousing, and the like" (Gal 5:19–21). The death of Jesus, our baptism, even the Christ within us has not simply destroyed all this. That is why Paul had to urge the Christians of Rome: "Let us cast off the works of darkness and put on the armor of light; let us conduct ourselves becomingly as in the day. . . . Put on the Lord Jesus Christ . . ." (Rom 13:12–14).

An Advent examination of conscience: What precisely are the areas of darkness within you? What keeps you from lighting up with the grace that is there? Does Christ radiate, shine forth, from your daily life? If not, why not? Is it that you are just "ordinary people,"[1] living the way your world expects you to live? Is there something of self you are clinging to, will not let go, even though it torments you? Is there a dark side of you that you refuse to face? Simply, how dark is your darkness, and why?

Besides the darkness in us, there is a darkness around us. As a Catholic theologian, I dare not suggest that this age after Christ is darker than the age before Christ. Still, it is unexpectedly dark. The Hebrews who hungered in the wilderness cannot compare with the billion who hunger right now. The destruction of Jerusalem by Nebuchadnezzar pales before the atomic wipe-out that leveled Nagasaki and Hiroshima. Never have the elderly been so lonely, so many of the young spaced out. The blind and the deaf and the lame, the lepers and the poor we read about in the Bible were blessed when set against the 200,000 inhumans who eat and sleep and defecate in the streets of Calcutta. Even Jesus could not walk safely in our cities. Why, three out of every four human beings would not recognize him!

After two thousand years, there is still a deep darkness in this redeemed world. Christ is here, for he has come. But the light that is Christ flickers and shines and blazes only through people, through Christians, through those who claim to follow him. What ever happened to the command of Christ: "Let your light so shine before men that they may see your good works and give glory to your Father who is in heaven" (Mt 5:16)? What ever happened to the plea of Paul: "Once you were darkness, but now you are light in the Lord; walk as children of light (for the fruit of light is found in all that is good and right and true), and try to learn what is pleasing to the Lord" (Eph 5:8-10)?

The day after Thanksgiving the *New York Times* told of a 33-year-old local cabdriver whose shoulder-length hair was tied in a ponytail. (Don't get distracted by the ponytail!) About five years ago, this cabby "prayed to God for guidance on how to help the forgotten people of the streets who exist in life's shadows." As he recalls it, God replied: "Make eight pounds of spaghetti, throw it in a pot, give it out on 103rd Street and Broadway with no conditions, and people will come." He did, they came, and now he goes from door to door giving people food to eat.[2]

I am not asking you to stuff the Big Apple with spaghetti. But a New York cabby can bring light into your Advent night. He prayed to a God who was there; he listened; he gave the simple gift God asked of him; he gave "with no conditions"; and people responded. Here is your Advent: Make the Christ who has come a reality, a living light, in your life and in some other life. Give of yourself . . . to one dark soul . . . with no conditions. Like the Christophers, light one candle in the darkness. Let Christ dawn!

St. Ignatius Loyola Church
New York City
November 30, 1980

2
PREPARE THE WAY OF THE LORD
Second Sunday of Advent (B)

- *Isaiah 40:1–5, 9–11*
- *2 Peter 3:8–14*
- *Mark 1:1–8*

You know, if the prophet Isaiah came back to earth today, he would not be happy with us Catholic homilists. We pay such scant attention to him, to any Sunday reading from the Old Testament. Oh yes, we make passing reference to it, at times link it to the Gospel reading. But very quickly we get on to the substantive stuff, the real good news, the New Testament.

And so it could be with Isaiah today (40:1–5, 9–11). How nice it is, how fortunate for us, that a voice cries from the council of heaven: "Make straight in the desert a highway for our God" (v. 3). How fortunate, for Mark applies the Isaian passage to John the Baptist and to Jesus: John is the "one crying in the wilderness," paving the way for Jesus (Mk 1:3). So, on to Mark, who will give us the real homiletic high. Isaiah has served his purpose: He has given Mark and me the handle we need.

Not so today, dear friends, not so today. On this second Sunday of Advent we shall focus on Isaiah. And right out of that last sentence my three points break forth: (1) Advent; (2) Isaiah; (3) we.

I

First, Advent. Here is our context, the liturgical framework within which a homily must make sense. Now both Isaiah and Mark sum up in a single word what the Church expects of us: "Prepare!"

23

(Isa 40:3; Mk 1:3). You know what it means to prepare: Get something ready beforehand, get yourself ready. A wedding shower or a birthday dinner, Halloween or a homily, nuclear war or intramural football, an economics exam or an economical date—you get ready for it. You don't just sit around waiting—as someone phrased it in a glorious blooper, you don't sit on your hands biting your fingernails.

But in Advent what are you preparing for? Simply, for the coming of Christ. Not for his first coming; that has come and gone. I cannot pretend that Christ has not yet come. Oh yes, in loving imagination I can take the last room in the Bethlehem Hilton, get in line at the stable, wonder when he's coming, stamp my frozen feet, check the gifts for the baby—blue booties or an Atari game. But only to reactivate what has already happened. I recall that unique coming of God in our flesh; but I recall it so that by memorializing it I may be carried out of myself to focus on a second coming, a final coming. On Christmas we shall proclaim the mystery of faith: Christ has come, Christ will come again! As the Letter to Titus puts it: We await "our blessed hope, the appearing of the glory of our great God and Savior Jesus Christ" (Tit 2:13).

II

But how do you prepare for "the Son of man coming on the clouds of heaven with power and great glory" (Mt 24:30)? It's so far off, unreal, hard to imagine. Even if the TV preachers have it taped, and Armageddon is a 200-mile battle line staring us in the face, how do you prepare? It's like preparing to be nuked. The same Letter to Titus has some concrete suggestions: "Renounce irreligion and worldly passions, live sober, upright, and godly lives in this world" (Tit 2:11). It's sound advice, any time of the day or night, any century. Worship God, cut down on the Schlitz and the sex, live like a man or woman redeemed by Christ's blood.

But that advice is too limited, too individualistic, for a people, a community that Christ has fashioned into his own body, has shaped to be an instrument of redemption. How does this *people* prepare? This is the question that drives me back to Isaiah.

You see, in this section of Isaiah (chapters 40–55) you have what scholars call the Book of the Consolation of Israel.[1] The year 587 had been a catastrophe for God's chosen people. Jerusalem and the Temple had been destroyed; all Judah was a shambles; thousands had been deported to Babylonia. The community was politically impotent, its public worship emasculated, its sacrifice a thing of the past. Justifiably, Isaiah calls the community in exile "a people robbed and plundered . . . trapped in holes and hidden in prison . . . a prey with none to rescue" (42:22). God's servant, Israel, was a horribly disfigured servant: "no form or comeliness . . . no beauty . . . despised and rejected . . . a man of sorrows and acquainted with grief" (53:2–3). And there were times when the exiles felt deep doubt: Has Yahweh failed His people? Are the gods of Babylon superior to our God?

And yet, even in exile Israel kept its faith alive, its law alive, its identity alive, its consciousness of continuity with the past—more alive than did their brothers and sisters back home in Jerusalem. Largely because of men like Isaiah.[2] Oh, he was brutally frank. He told the exiles why the Lord had let this happen. It was His judgment on Israel: "You have burdened me with your sins, you have wearied me with your iniquities" (43:24). It is for their infidelity that they have "drunk of the Lord's wrath, drunk to the dregs the bowl of staggering" (51:17). That is why "devastation and destruction, famine and sword" have laid them low (51:19).

Brutal indeed; and still Isaiah can console the exiles. Their exile is not so much God's vengeance as the people's purification. God tells Isaiah: "Comfort, comfort my people. . . . Speak tenderly to Jerusalem," cry to her that her exile is almost over, "that her iniquity is pardoned" (40:1–2); she is totally forgiven. And not simply an impersonal word: "Behold, *the Lord comes* with might. . . . He will feed His flock like a shepherd, gather the lambs in His arms, carry them in His bosom, and gently lead those that are with young" (40:10–11). He will bring them back to Jerusalem, back home, back to a restored Temple.

More astonishingly still, Israel is not saved simply for her own sake. Isaiah makes clear that Israel is a people with a mission, a mission to the world, to bring Yahweh's redemption and salvation to all humankind. Through Israel His holiness will be manifested, and the nations will recognize that Yahweh alone is God.

But take notice: The Israel that bears this vocation is not the great nation ruled by King David. It is the "remnant," the "poor" of Yahweh who despite crushing obstacles have remained faithful, keep the law in their hearts, serve Yahweh and Him alone, hope only in Him. It is through suffering that Israel becomes a source of salvation. And there is more suffering ahead. The innocent will suffer that the guilty may repent and escape judgment. The mission of service will never die in Israel; she *is* a suffering servant.

Briefly, Israel's exile was purification from sin and preparation for a mission. In His own good time God would come, a God who forgave the infidelity of His people, a God who even then was readying them through suffering to be a redemptive people, to bear suffering witness to Yahweh, to be a people of hope.

III

And what of us? I suggest that our Catholic community is experiencing its own Babylon. Two decades ago we Catholic Americans seemed to have it "made." In a confused world, we were maddeningly sure of what we believed. In a carnal culture, we preached an asceticism not of earth. In a country of a thousand gods, our worship was pure, recognizable the world over, satisfyingly dull, one and the same for every one of us. We had an enormous school system, staffed by sisters garbed in every color of the rainbow; we had more priests than we could use. We even had political clout—with labor and management, with government and society. One of our boys had made it to the White House. We were accepted by the culture.

Almost overnight, all that has changed. In a sense, we are dispersed, in exile. We are not the same unified people that overcame so many enemies—the No Nothings and the Nativists, the Ku Klux Klan, the establishments in New York and Boston. The old identity tags are gone: fish on Friday and frequent confession, novenas and Benediction and the Rosary, sexual standards and dogmatic intransigeance, fidelity to Rome and to marriage vows, Lenten penance and Latin Mass. We find it hard to say with certainty what it means to be Catholic. What makes us different? Are we still a single people? Thousands have left us, or don't care any longer. Our enemies find us gratifyingly divided, and politicos don't have to promise us much. We are a people in dispersion. Has the Lord failed us? Or is He punishing us for infidelity?

My friends, I am not Isaiah—and so I dare not propose a theology of God's dealings with the American Church. But this I do say. Like the Israelites in Babylonia, (1) we start from where we are, (2) we must be made conscious of a mission, and (3) that mission involves a suffering servant. A word on each.

We start from where we are. We are indeed struggling—struggling to find ourselves, to uncover what makes us profoundly one, in the way we think, the way we act, the way we worship. Here I recall the prophetic wisdom of that remarkable Jesuit John Courtney Murray at the close of the Second Vatican Council: "As was the experience of Vatican II, so must be the postconciliar experience: the contemporary Catholic, like the bishops at the Council, must begin with a good deal of confusion and uncertainty, will therefore pass through a period of anxiety and tension, but can expect to end with a certain measure of light and of joy."

I lived through the more placid years—lived placidly myself. But I fear that we had gotten too fat, too content. Paradoxically, we accepted the culture uncritically *and* were largely walled off from the world's concerns. For all our present problems, I find the Church more Christlike today. We are more acutely aware of ourselves as a pilgrim people who never have it "made" in this life, more agonizingly aware of our brothers and sisters crying to heaven for justice and bread. We have a fresh vision of what it means to be church—not as clear as theologians would like, but in its very openness terribly exciting.

But what we desperately need is to be made conscious of a mission. Neither in Dahlgren nor across the country can we Catholics be a self-contained enclave, living for ourselves and the integrity of "the one true Church." If we are Jesus' disciples, then his challenge is addressed to us: "You are the salt of the earth. . . . You are the light of the world" (Mt 5:13–14). Our lives should season our culture, spice it with God's gospel. Our lives should "so shine before men and women that they may see [our] good works and give glory to [our] Father who is in heaven" (v. 16).

It would be impossible if the "good works" Jesus demanded were deeds of power and majesty, if we had to witness to the world in philosophical wisdom or three-point homilies. No, the power of God is the folly of the cross (cf. 1 Cor 1:18). "Consider your call," Paul commands. "Not many of you were wise according to worldly standards, not many were powerful, not many were of noble birth; but God chose what is foolish in the world to shame the wise; God chose what is weak in the world to shame the strong; God chose what is low and despised in the world, even things that are not, to bring to nothing things that are, so that no human being might boast in the presence of God" (1 Cor 1:26–29).

Like Israel in exile, our covenant community is called to be a suffering servant. We servants are no greater than our Master. If the world is redeemed by the folly of a cross, it is the crucifixion not of the Head alone but of the whole body. You need not carve new crosses, clothe yourself with camel's hair and eat locusts, give up the Pub for little Jesus' sake. The cross is all around you, in this mad world and on your crazy street. The cross is inside you, in the challenge to live your faith to the full, to make your Christian life the life of Christ, to "be perfect as your heavenly Father is perfect" (Mt 5:48). The cross is our Catholic community: how to remain one when so much drives us apart, how to swallow our own "rights" for the good of the group, how to let go of a past that is personally precious, how to love one another when we don't like one another.

There is much to do in our wilderness to prepare for the Lord's coming. What keeps us from despair, what keeps us a people of hope, is the Christian paradox: He who is to come is already here. He is in your midst, in your heart, on your altar. That is why you can do the impossible: You can dance with a cross on your back.

Dahlgren Chapel
Georgetown University
December 6, 1981

3
SHALL WE LOOK FOR ANOTHER?
Third Sunday of Advent (A)

- *Isaiah 35:1–6, 10*
- *James 5:7–10*
- *Matthew 11:2–11*

Today's Gospel (Mt 11:2–11) worries me. Let me share my worry with you. In three stages, of course. First, what is it that the Gospel tells us? Second, why does it create a problem? Third, what can we say to the problem?

I

First then, what does the Gospel tell us? It tells us that John the Baptist, in his prison cell, was puzzled. Like many another, he expected the Messiah to be a fiery social reformer, Elijah come to earth again. He doesn't quite see this in Jesus, but he isn't sure. And so he sends his disciples to ask Jesus: Are you the promised Messiah, or do we have to look elsewhere? Jesus does not come out with a flat yes. He invites John to answer his own question. He tells his questioners: Look around and see for yourselves. Remember the prediction of Isaiah, the works the Messiah will perform at his coming:

> Then the eyes of the blind shall be opened,
>   and the ears of the deaf unstopped;
> then shall the lame man leap like a hart,
>   and the tongue of the dumb leap for joy.
>
> (Isa 35:5–6)

29

In that light, Jesus says: "Go and tell John what you hear and see: the blind receive their sight and the lame walk, lepers are cleansed and the deaf hear, the dead are raised up and the poor have good news preached to them" (Mt 11:4–5).

Very simply, Jesus answers John: Do you want to know if the Christ has come? Look around you: The signs are there, for all to see.

II

Now why does this Gospel create a problem? I can put it in the pungent challenge of a sympathetic Jew: "We must . . . question, in the light of the Bible, whether the message of the Old Testament which the New Testament claims has been fulfilled, has in fact been fulfilled in history. . . . And here, my dear Christian readers, we give a negative reply. We can see no kingdom and no peace and no redemption."[1]

The problem the Gospel raises is this: If an unbeliever were to ask you for evidence that the Messiah has come, what signs would you point to? In response to our Jewish friend, where is the kingdom, the peace, the redemption promised in the Old Testament? If you believe, with the Preface for the feast of Christ the King, that the kingdom of Christ is "a kingdom of truth and life, a kingdom of holiness and grace, a kingdom of justice, love, and peace," where is it? Can these be the Messianic times? When three out of every four human beings do not know Christ? When one out of four goes to bed hungry? When violence is a way of life? When whole countries lie enslaved? When Christians wage war on Christians? When six million of God's chosen people die in gas ovens? *This* is the new covenant in Christ's blood? This is "the day of the Lord"? This is a world redeemed from sin? This is what the Old Testament was preparing for? Can you say, "Look around you: as the heavens proclaim the glory of God, so the earth proclaims the coming of Christ"?

III

A problem indeed. What can we say to it? As your in-house theologian, I can say two things right off. First, the kingdom of Christ is not here purely and simply; it *is* here and it is *not* here. As

Vatican II put it, the Church "becomes on earth the initial budding forth of that kingdom."[2] We are still fashioning the kingdom, the rule of Christ over human hearts; and we fashion the kingdom through tears and trembling, through sin and selfishness, through suffering and death. We are indeed a pilgrim people. Second, the most significant facets of Christ's kingdom are invisible, beyond the power of sense to perceive. The same Jesus who declared that "the kingdom of heaven is at hand" (Mt 4:17) insisted that "the kingdom of God is within you" (Lk 17:21).[3] It is, above all else, "a kingdom of holiness and grace."

This may help, but it does not completely satisfy. Even though God's kingdom has not been totally established, even though God's rule is primarily over our hidden hearts, it should reveal its effects now, in our everyday world of flesh and blood. My theology explains why the Church is not perfect; it does not explain why the Church is not holier than it is, why Christians are not more visible sacraments to the world, more transparent signs that Christ is here. It does not explain how so many in a redeemed world can be as ruthless, as pitiless, as loveless as the pagans St. Paul castigated.

Advent lays an awesome responsibility on Christians. Ever since Christ took his smile and his tears from our earth, it is we who have to let the world see that he-who-is-to-come has actually come, that he is still here. *We* are the works that reveal him—or conceal him. Not all can reveal him as radically as did Dorothy Day, who died last week at 83. From jails and soup kitchens, through the *Catholic Worker* and houses of hospitality, in voluntary poverty and with unconfined faith, she gave her life literally to the poor and the destitute, lived and ate with these down-and-out images of Christ. At her funeral, former yippee Abbie Hoffman remarked: "She is the nearest thing this Jewish boy is ever going to get to a saint." And in the overflow outside the church, "a drifter who gave his name as Lazarus" said "with tears oozing down his seamed cheeks: 'That fine lady gave me love.' "[4]

No, you cannot all be "street saints." But you can be Christian; you must be. And that means you give love; it means you shape Christ's kingdom, make him "the king of hearts"—of your heart first. It calls for constant conversion, perhaps radical reform, so that whether playing or praying, laughing or weeping, dancing or working, living or dying, Christ shines forth from you. If not you, who? If not now, when? If not here, where?

In a few moments we shall be privileged to share in a twin ceremony: We shall receive two young ladies into our community of faith. By a happy coincidence, both are named Allison; one is a fresh-born child, the other a graduate student. One Allison will be baptized, the other will profess her faith and be confirmed.

Each Allison symbolizes in her own way the problem this homily has wrestled with. The child will tell us mutely that the kingdom of God is largely invisible; for God will take possession of her soul without her seeing it, without her knowing it, without her asking it—somewhat as He tented in the heart of Mary at the first moment of her becoming. The adult will tell us with deliberate conviction that she has discovered Christ in his Church, that she has found signs of his presence in our community, that here she glimpses his kingdom, his peace, his redemption. Each Allison will become, in St. Paul's words, "a new creation; the old has passed away; behold, the new has come" (2 Cor 5:17).

This is what Advent is all about: He-who-is-to-come comes to two human hearts. Please God, you and I will recognize him as waters of grace flow on one Allison and words of grace flow from the other. Please God, these will be signs for us, a moving reminder that these two children of God represent what you and I are trying to live, and a dazzling proof that, for all the apparent absence of Christ, he is really present here.

Dahlgren Chapel
Georgetown University
December 14, 1980

4
ON TIPTOE OF EXPECTATION
Third Sunday of Advent (C)

- *Zephaniah 3:14–18*
- *Philippians 4:4–7*
- *Luke 3:10–18*

There is something paradoxical about Advent. Some might even call it a contradiction. Advent is a season of waiting—waiting for Jesus; and yet he is already here. Zephaniah exhorts you to "sing aloud . . . shout . . . rejoice and exult with all your heart" because "the king of Israel, the Lord, is *in your midst* (Zeph 3:14–15); but Paul commands you to "rejoice [because] the Lord is *at hand*" (Phil 4:4–5), his second coming is *near.* Luke tells us "the people were on tiptoe of expectation" (Lk 3:15 NEB), were wondering if the Baptist might be the Christ; but we know he is not, we know the Christ, have experienced him. Well, is Christ here or isn't he? And if he is, why stand a-tiptoe with expectation?

There is indeed a paradox here, but not a contradiction. The paradox stems from a tension intrinsic to human and Christian existence. I mean the tension between a twin reality, two facets of human and Christian living: yes and no, here and not here, already and not yet, possession and waiting, we have and we don't have. My point is, Advent is not simply a season; the whole of life is an Advent: We are waiting expectantly for something that in some sense is already here.

This paradox, this problem—our life as Advent—seems best approached in three stages. First, the human yes-and-no, the human already-and-not-yet, the human expectancy. Second, the Christian yes-and-no, the Christian already-and-not-yet, the Christian expectancy. Third, the question asked of John by the soldiers and tax collectors: "What shall we do?" (Lk 3:12, 14).

I

First then, the human yes-and-no, the human already-and-not-yet, the human expectancy. Simply as human beings, simply as men and women, we wait ceaselessly for something that in some sense is already here. Take the four seasons of human living: childhood and adolescence, early adulthood, the middle years, old age.[1] Each season is indeed different, but each contains within itself both the past and the future. Whatever your age—20, 40, 60, or beyond—you have within you the seeds of what you will be tomorrow. For better or worse, like it or not, you are now very much what you will be. And still there is room for growth, for change. You are already a person, but not yet. For life is process: You are at once the same as you were yesterday and different. "You haven't changed a bit" is not always a compliment; more importantly, it's never quite true. Not true of your flesh or your spirit; not true of your mind or your heart, your intelligence or your love. It's a soul-shivering paradox: You are now what you will be, and still what you will be is so much fuller, so much more completely you, than what you are now.

And so you will struggle, you will gasp for breath and shout for joy, you will be very vulnerable and unexpectedly strong, you will work and play, rock and roll, love and hate, hope and despair, ripen and wither—and through it all you will fashion ever more fully the person you already are. Even old age will not be death, unless you make it so; old age too is a movement, through kenosis to contemplation, through self-emptying to a long loving look at the real.

In a word, human living is an advent: You are constantly coming to be. At one and the same time you are and you are not; you wait "on tiptoe of expectation" for what is yet to be.

II

Second, the Christian yes-and-no, the Christian already-and-not-yet, the Christian expectancy. I mean the paradox that runs all through our Christian experience: We are waiting a-tiptoe for what in some sense, to some extent, is already here. Nineteen hundred and fifty years ago Jesus proclaimed "The kingdom of God is at hand" (Mk 1:15), and still we pray "Thy kingdom come." Indeed God's reign over our hearts was inaugurated by Christ's coming, but we ceaselessly pray "that God's universal reign be established—that destiny toward which the whole of time is directed."[2] God's dominion over us and over the world is still imperfect. Look at Cambodia and Iran, look at South Africa and Northern Ireland, look at your own city, your own corridor, your own heart. The kingdom will not come until Jesus comes again. Oh yes, the Church of Christ is, as Vatican II saw, "the seed and beginning" of the kingdom Jesus proclaimed; and still the Church is not purely and simply the kingdom of God. The Church "yearns for, gasps for, strains towards the kingdom in its perfection, its consummation."[3]

In like manner, you and I. We are indeed redeemed through the blood of Christ; and still, as St. Paul put it so movingly, "we who have the first fruits of the Spirit groan inwardly as we wait for adoption as sons and daughters, the redemption of our bodies" (Rom 8:23), of our whole selves wholly. Indeed our sins are forgiven us; and still we remain sinners, discouragingly sinful, prey to so much devilish seduction, working out our salvation in fear and trembling. You are remarkably holy, each and all of you; for in grace Father, Son, and Spirit make their home within you; where two or three of you are gathered in Christ's name, there he is in the midst of you; at peak moments you feel him, experience his presence; in a few short moments you will throne him in your hand, pillow him on your tongue, nestle him in your flesh. And still your God is a hidden God; with Paul, "now we see in a mirror dimly, but then face to face" (1 Cor 13:12). God is here, but not as He will be. No wonder St. John wrote: "Beloved, we are God's children now; it does not yet appear what we shall be, but we know that when He appears we shall be like Him, for we shall see Him as He is" (1 Jn 3:2).

III

So much for Burghardt the psychologist, so much for Burghardt the theologian: Human life and Christian life, each is a waiting "on tiptoe of expectation" for something that in some sense, to some extent, is already here. Now prepare ye for Burghardt the moralist. It is the question you must be waiting for (if not on tip-

toe), the question asked of the Baptist by the soldiers and tax collectors: "What shall we do?" While we're waiting, what shall we
do?

I have one swift answer: Live in hope! Both words are important, indispensable, irreplaceable: "hope" and "live." You must be
men and women of ceaseless hope, because only tomorrow can today's human and Christian promise be realized; and every tomorrow will have its own tomorrow, world without end. Every human
act, every Christian act, is an act of hope. But that means you must
be men and women of the present, you must live this moment—
really live it, not just endure it—because this very moment, for all
its imperfection and frustration, *because* of its imperfection and
frustration, is pregnant with all sorts of possibilities, is pregnant
with the future, is pregnant with love, is pregnant with Christ.

If your dream is the dance, by all means point your toes towards Kennedy Center; but today you point them down, on a
dusty, creaking wood; today is the ballet bar and the mirror, the extra job and the endless pliés. But each plié should be an affirmation
of life, each plié an act of hope.

If you're a student on the great American grade chase, if for
you Georgetown is simply a stepping stone to future success, if December is one sleepless memory lesson, my heart goes out to you.
Not because your blue eyes are circled in black, but because you
are not *living* today. You might remember, an American law forbids
force-feeding a goose to produce a rich liver pâté.

If you've discovered, to your dismay, what you are not, know
that in this discovery you are beginning to discover who you are.
There is so much to you, human and divine, if you but open your
eyes to see. More glorious still, there is so much more you can be,
if you but open your heart to God and to the images of God, if you
but live who you are.

If you're plagued by your sinfulness, if guilt paralyzes or
shakes you, if you are not as Christlike as you ought to be and you
quiver with fear, put your hope not in yourself or your suitemate or
your spouse, but in God, a forgiving God who does not want the
death of the sinner but that you should live. Today is rich in hope,
because today God forgives.

If life is tough, if you hurt in head or heart, if love has forsaken
you, if God's ways seem inhuman ways, don't just endure it in the
hope that tomorrow may be more tolerable. *Live* today's agony;

work through it; if you can, put your hand trustingly in the Lord's; cry out, if you must, against God or man. Only, don't blot out today's darkness. It might help to recall what the distinguished historian Charles A. Beard said in his last class at Columbia. Asked what he had learned after fifty years of teaching, he responded: "Number one, when it is dark enough, you can see the stars...."[4] It reminds me of a Japanese haiku, where a poor fellow, stripped of all he owns, says very simply: "My house burned down last night. Now I can see the moon."

The applications are legion, yet only you know intimately what keeps you from living in hope. But whoever you are, if you want to lift Advent from liturgy to life, don't waste your todays with sheer waiting. Wait indeed, for tomorrow promises to be rich in life and love. But life and love are here today, because God is here today— because your brothers and sisters are here today.

I leave for your meditation a paragraph from a profound Protestant theologian, Reinhold Niebuhr: "Nothing that is worth doing can be achieved in our lifetime; therefore we must be saved by hope. Nothing which is true or beautiful or good makes complete sense in any immediate context of history; therefore we must be saved by faith. Nothing we do, however virtuous, can be accomplished alone; therefore we are saved by love. No virtuous act is quite as virtuous from the standpoint of our friend or foe as it is from our standpoint. Therefore we must be saved by the final form of love which is forgiveness."[5]

Dahlgren Chapel
Georgetown University
December 16, 1979

LISTEN LISTEN LISTEN LISTEN LISTEN LISTEN LISTEN LISTEN

LENT

5
FOR YOUR LENTEN PENANCE, LISTEN
Second Sunday of Lent (A)

- *Genesis 12:1–4*
- *2 Timothy 1:8–10*
- *Matthew 17:1–9*

Today's Transfiguration scene (Mt 17:1–9) is packed with majesty and mystery. There is so much to fill the homilist, like the disciples, with awe. Do you remember the experience of Moses on Mount Sinai (Exod 24:15–18; 34:29–35)? Well, the events of Sinai are re-enacted in the experience of the new Moses. Like the first Moses, Jesus too goes up a mountain. His face too shines unbearably. A cloud covers this mountain too, a luminous cloud, the symbol of God's presence. Here too God speaks from the cloud. Even the three booths or tents Peter wants to set up recall the Feast of Tabernacles or Booths that commemorated the sojourn of the Israelites on Sinai while they received the revelation of the law through Moses.

And here we go beyond Sinai. Here Moses and Elias represent the law and the prophets; their presence bears witness that in Jesus the law and the prophets are fulfilled. And here we meet that astounding paradox: To be Messiah meant to suffer, and still Jesus was the glorious Son of Man.

There is just too much—even for three points! And so I shall focus on one facet of that majestic mystery. I shall concentrate on a single word spoken by the Father to Peter, James, and John: "Listen" (Mt 17:5). I shall ask you to listen in three directions: Listen to one another; listen to Jesus; listen to the world around you.

41

I

I suggest you begin by listening to one another. It's not at all easy. Listening is an arduous art. You see, most conversations are not conversations at all. Either they are monologues: I wait patiently until you have finished—since civility demands it—and then I say exactly what I would have said if you had not spoken. Or they are debates: I do indeed listen, but only for that inept word or false phrase at which I proceed to intercept and destroy. No, to listen is to give yourself totally, for that moment or that day, to another, to put yourself into the other's mind, yes the other's heart. It means that you hear not naked words but a human person.

Some of the most remarkable people in history have been great listeners. Remember the mother of Jesus? Luke tells us that she "kept all these things, pondering them in her heart" (Lk 2:19; see 2:51): She had listened to shepherds telling of angels. Recall Helen Keller, blind, deaf, mute, "listening" to Anne Sullivan as if her life depended on it (it did indeed). Think of St. John Vianney, the famous parish priest of Ars in France: Twelve hours a day in the confessional, he listened—not simply to sins but to fractured hearts. And I shall never forget a remarkable scholar of early Christianity at Catholic University, Johannes Quasten. He used to say to us with quiet sincerity: "I learn as much from my students as my students learn from me."

The problem is, to listen is to risk. It takes your precious time, often when you can least afford it. You take on other people's problems, when you have enough of your own. It means getting involved. For if you listen, you open yourself: to your children or "the help," to subordinates or (God save the mark!) students. If you're a good listener, people "dump" on you. If you listen, someone may fall in love with you—and that can a burden you do not care to bear.

But the risk will be matched by a matchless joy. For listening, really listening, is an act of love; and so it is wonderfully human, splendidly Christian. Love far more than knowledge, I assure you. I used to think, in my youthful arrogance, that what I had to offer the Catholic world was a hatful of answers. No, I come to others as I am, with my own ignorance, my own weakness, my own sinfulness, my own fears and tears. I share not words but myself; I am there. Not my ear or my tongue; simply I. And that, dear friends, is

my Christian mission and yours: to be where another can reach out
to us.

II

Second, listen to Jesus. This is the command of the Father
from the cloud: "Listen to him" (Mt 17:5). This is what the favored
three were ordered to do. Why? Because here is at once God's Son
and God's Revelation. Here is the prophet par excellence. He himself is the Word, the Word enfleshed, the Word God speaks, the
Word beyond compare.

This is not pious poetry; it is profound truth. The breath-taking "new thing" in God's self-disclosure is the opening sentence in
the Epistle to the Hebrews: "In many and various ways God spoke
of old to our fathers by the prophets; but in these last days He has
spoken to us by a Son" (Heb 1:1–2). In the new covenant God expresses Himself in a Word that is itself a Person. The personal
Word God utters from eternity, He uttered on a midnight clear—
to us. Jesus *is* God's revelation to us; he is the point of personal
contact between God and us.

How does Jesus speak to us? Vatican II rings loud and clear:
"[Christ] is present in his word, since it is he himself who speaks
when the holy Scriptures are read in the church."[1] Do you believe
that? Do you really believe "This is the word of the Lord"? If you
do, how do you listen to him? As breathlessly as Moses listened to
the Lord on Sinai? As open to God's word as was the teen-age virgin of Nazareth? Do you "marvel," like his townspeople, "at the
words of grace" that fall from Jesus' lips (Lk 4:22)? Or has repeti-
tion dulled your appetite, and Christ is less charismatic than Kotter, J. C. less exciting than J. R.?[2]

The thrilling fact is, this Jesus who speaks to you is not a char-
acter out of a dead past. Listening to Scripture in the liturgy is not
the same as reading Augustine's *Confessions* or Gibran's *Prophet*, not
the same as hearing a Shakespeare sonnet or Handel's *Messiah*.
When the New Testament is read to you, Jesus himself speaks to
you. Now. Here is the risen Christ, incomparably alive, opening up
to you the meaning of what you are hearing, as he did to the deso-
late disciples on the road to Emmaus. And as you listen, you too
can exclaim as they exclaimed: "Did not our hearts burn within us
while he talked to us . . . while he opened to us the Scriptures?" (Lk

24:32). But for that, your hearts have to be open. You have to say, with Samuel of old, "Speak, Lord, for thy servant heareth" (1 Sam 3:9, 10).

But again, there is something distinctive here. Listening to Jesus is not the same as listening to others. The same intensity, yes, the same openness; but a greater risk. When the Father told Peter, James, and John "Listen to him," he was saying "Obey him; do what he tells you; follow him." To listen to Jesus is to be his disciple, to listen the way Abraham listened to the Lord and left his "country and kindred and [his] father's house" (Gen 12:1–4). Is this how you let Scripture speak to you? Are you saying "Speak, Lord, for thy servant heareth," or do you really mean, as the Protestant ethicist Paul Ramsey rephrased it, "Speak, Lord, and thy servant will think it over"?

If you really listen to Jesus in the proclaimed word, you have a fair chance of hearing him in your everyday life. Not a vision, I assure you, but Jesus speaking in your heart as truly as anyone you love profoundly speaks to your heart.

III

Let me develop this a bit in my third point: Listen to the world around you. I have insisted that when the Scriptures are read to you, God speaks to you; and that is a thrilling truth. More thrilling still is that our God is not imprisoned in a book, even in a book of His own inspiring. God is ceaselessly speaking to us. The problem is, we are dreadfully deaf to His voice.

To begin with, God speaks to me through things, the things He has shaped. The Psalmist was right: "The heavens are telling the glory of God, and the firmament proclaims His handiwork. Day to day pours forth speech, and night to night declares knowledge" (Ps 19:1–2). For God could fashion nothing unless it imaged some perfection of His. There is no blade of grass that does not speak of Him. The whirlwinds reflect His power, the mountains mirror His majesty, surging waves His irresistibleness, a star-flecked sky His breath-taking loveliness. And if I miss their message, it is because I am not tuned into God, am not listening.

God speaks to me through history, through human events. The cry of the blacks for freedom was a cry of God, a cry to "let [His] people go." From the ovens and gas chambers of Dachau, the

God of Abraham, Isaac, and Jacob is talking to a world that would like to forget its inhumanity to Jewish man. (Last year a Georgetown student declared that the Holocaust never happened.) From Appalachia to Calcutta it is the voice of Jesus that begs for bread and human dignity. But I need him to put his fingers into my ears and murmur "Be opened" (Mk 7:33–34).

Very importantly, God speaks to me through *my* history. Yesterday, in Boston, I buried a young friend half my age. Seven years ago I presided at his wedding; yesterday I consigned his cancerous flesh to the earth. For three days I have been tempted to complain with Martha, "Lord, if you had [really] been here, [our] brother would not have died" (Jn 11:21). I cannot understand it. "Here," I said in my homily, "here is a young man ... highly intelligent, good in the strong sense of the word, shaped in equal parts of humor and love. In a world bent by anger and hate, by ambition and suspicion, he is remarkably open and friendly, generous and trusting, a wonderful welding of karate and gentleness. And he loves—loves God and people, loves wife and life—dear God, how passionately in love he is with life! And without warning life is stolen from him. Not swiftly and painlessly; no, slowly and cruelly. So once again, as with my brother wasting away at 27, as with a score of black Atlanta lads, I cannot help asking: Lord, where were you? When he whom you loved was dying, where were you?"[3]

Only by listening, almost in desperation, do I hear God speaking. Not explaining, not defending, not justifying. Only, "Do you love me? Then trust me. I do care. I was never closer to Joe than in those last agonizing months. For every Gethsemane is *my* garden, and every Calvary is *my* cross."

Dear friends in Christ: If you want to "do" something for Lent, if you want to share in the dying/rising of Jesus, skip the Scarsdale diet; forget the carrots and the cottage cheese, the fresh apple and the Tab. Simply listen: Listen to one another, listen to Jesus in the proclaimed word, listen to the word of God in the world around you. For your Lenten penance, please ... listen.

Dahlgren Chapel
Georgetown University
March 15, 1981

6
FORGIVE US AS WE FORGIVE
Fourth Sunday of Lent (C)

- *Josue 5:9–12*
- *2 Corinthians 5:17–21*
- *Luke 15:1–3, 11–32*

Seven years ago, that remarkable psychiatrist Karl Menninger produced a heady volume entitled *Whatever Became of Sin?*[1] At a time when the word "sin" was dropping out of our Catholic vocabulary, a distinguished therapist was not afraid to speak of it. In fact, he did not hestitate to quote the First Epistle of John: "If we say we have no sin, we deceive ourselves, and the truth is not in us" (1 Jn 1:8).

Today's parable of the prodigal, at the midpoint of Lent, reintroduces us to sin. To much more indeed—to the unforgettable forgiveness of a father; but even that forgiveness does not reveal its richness unless we grasp, however feebly, what it is that is forgiven. So, let's look at sin, at the prodigal in all of us. Those of you who see no parallel, those of you who find in yourselves the elder son who "never disobeyed" (Lk 15:29)—well, you can distract yourselves by wondering enviously whether we sinners have had more fun than you saints!

Three stages to my development, three questions. First, what is this thing called sin? Second, how do we Christians touch forgiveness to sin? Third, what does the parable tell us about God? Sin . . . forgiveness . . . God.

I

First then, what is this thing called sin? Here God's own word is expressive.[2] In the Old Testament, to sin is not merely to miss the mark; it is not only to be quite human, to fall short of what God and our brothers and sisters have a right to expect of us. That is all very true; it is what we are all like—we all fall short. But this is altogether negative. Once Israel came to know God, sin was seen as rebellion. From the first man's sin to the whole nation's sin, to sin was to revolt, to rebel, to disobey. And the rebellion, though it could mean trampling on the rights of fellow humans, was at bottom and basically, ultimately and primarily rebellion against God. It meant deliberately, consciously, knowingly to resist the will of God, to flout His law. The first man sinned in that Adam ate of the tree "of which I commanded you, 'You shall not eat of it' " (Gen 3:17). David, adulterous murderer, finally recognized that he had not only violated the rights of Uriah: "I have sinned against *the Lord*" (1 Sam 12:13). And sin for the nation, for Israel, meant to play the harlot, to be unfaithful to God; it meant to break a covenant, to offend against a personal God.

The New Testament builds on the Old. St. Paul speaks of Sin with a capital S, an evil force that tyrannizes each of us, a power hostile to God, a force that alienates from God. For St. John, sin is separation from God, the hostility of a man or woman against a God who would save them. And St. Luke's parable of the prodigal suggests vividly what it really means to sin. To sin, as the prodigal sinned, is not primarily to squander a father's wealth; to fornicate, as the prodigal fornicated, is a symptom of something more profound. To sin is to break a bond, to destroy a relationship, to withdraw *myself* from God my Father and from His love. The confession of the prodigal is pregnant: "Father, I have sinned against heaven and before you; I am no longer worthy to be called your son" (Lk 15:21).

Few sins, however, are aimed directly at God. Rarely do we set up what we know are false gods; rarely if ever do we curse God in cold blood. More often we offend God by offending against the images of God, against the men and women shaped by God to His likeness. Most sins reflect the sin of Cain, who turned on his brother Abel and slew him. Most sins exemplify man's inhumanity to man.

That inhumanity takes place on national, global, cosmic levels. Two world wars took over 25 million lives. Two atomic bombs fashioned fresh hells in Hiroshima and Nagasaki. Nazi gas chambers exterminated six million Jews. Napalm converted Vietnam into family incinerators. Blood reddens the flesh of Afghans and Africans, of Arabs and Jews, of northern Irish and Latin Americans. Poverty beds a billion human beings hungry each night. Half of Cambodia is dead. In a single year, 50 million abortions.

But I dare not lay sin solely on communists, find sin only in the heart of Iranians or the I.R.A., blame it all on the heads of state. "If we say *we* have no sin . . . the truth is not in us." I do not say we have destroyed the covenant that links us to God; such radical sin is surely rare in our lives. Rather we are Christian schizophrenics; we are inwardly rent, each of us two persons. We do not hurl at God a definitive no, do not really reject Him; at bottom, we love Him; and so, in harmony with the promise of Christ, God loves us and lives within us. But we do not live out the logic of that dynamic divine presence. We play games with God. We neither embrace Him totally nor repulse Him completely—and that is a dangerous line to walk, a perilous tightrope.

It was the ceaseless sin of the Israelites as denounced by the Lord through Jeremiah: "You have played the harlot with many lovers; and would you return to me?" (Jer 3:1). It is the recurring sin of Christians whenever we try to serve two masters. We compromise. We crawl to the edge of sin-unto-death . . . but not quite over. And so you have that endless catalog of "venial" sins—I disobeyed, I lied, I gossiped, I cursed, I got angry, I drank too much, I stole, I cheated—repeated so often that I question my own sincerity. You have that smaller list of "serious" sins—from lust through prodigal waste to our whole life style—which are not "unto death" for me only because I did not quite know what I was doing. And most importantly, you have that set of sins impossible to catalog— sins of "omission"—impossible to catalog because in each instance I did . . . nothing. A child was starving, and I closed my eyes; napalm fired human flesh, and I said not a word; slum landlords gouged the helpless, and I exclaimed "Isn't that terrible!"; public officials betrayed their sacred trust, and I thought "Everybody does it"; a stranger asked a smile, and I never gave it.

"If we say *we* have no sin . . . the truth is not in us."

II

My second point, my second question: How do we Christians touch forgiveness to sin? A pertinent question where sin is concerned. For day after day we pray to our Father a perilous prayer: "Forgive us our sins *as we forgive* those who sin against us." And all the while we find it so hard to forgive others, to forgive ourselves, to accept forgiveness.

It is not easy to forgive others. Not if my own experience is typical. Oh yes, I can forgive the Russians for raping Afghanistan; I can forgive Richard Nixon for letting John Dean "twist slowly in the wind"; I can forgive Pontius Pilate for washing his hands of Jesus Christ. But those sins do not cut me personally. What of the bishop who banned me from his diocese? What of the hidebound Catholics who publicly question my fidelity to the Church? I hurt quickly and I forgive slowly. Even when I do forgive, I can make the "sinner" feel awfully uncomfortable, let him "twist in the wind" awhile—for his own good, of course. And there are "elder brother" genes in most of us: We don't approve of parties for *other* repentant sinners; not if we've been fairly faithful recently.

It is not easy to forgive ourselves. Not if my own experience is typical. The imperfection I expect of others I will not tolerate in myself. The sinfulness I find so human in you I reproach as inhuman in myself. Guilt hounds me agonizingly long. For all too many, the ego is a harsh taskmaster. I ask you what I must often ask myself: Why are you so hard on yourself?

It is not easy to accept forgiveness. Whether it's God who whispers "Your sins are forgiven you," or a priest who murmurs "I absolve you," or a friend who waves away our apologies "Oh, forget it," we won't let go. We keep clutching what has been forgiven; we hark back to what has been forgotten. I don't know why. Perhaps forgiveness, like love, lays too heavy a burden on us; it demands a response. If love calls for loving, forgiveness calls for giving: I must open myself to another. And that calls for courage: I leave myself vulnerable; I can be horribly hurt.

Whatever the reasons, we Christians are creatures of contradiction. Without forgiveness we could not be Christians; and still we are so slow to forgive others, to forgive ourselves, to accept forgiveness. Perhaps it is time to turn to God.

III

My third point, therefore, my third question: What does the parable of the prodigal tell us about God? It tells in striking imagery what the Gospels proclaim time and again: Our God is not a God of vengeance, He is a God who forgives. Not from some distant star; God took and wore our sin-scarred flesh. Not by words alone, "Go in peace"; to atone for sin, God died in frightful agony—for you, for me. The prodigal reminds us that there is "more joy in heaven over one sinner who repents than over ninety-nine righteous who need no repentance" (Lk 15:7). It recalls the last discourse of Jesus: "No longer do I call you servants. . . . I have called you friends" (Jn 15:15). It recalls St. Paul: "If while we were enemies we were reconciled to God by the death of His Son, much more, now that we are reconciled, shall we be saved by his life" (Rom 5:10). It suggests that grace is stronger than sin, that God's life in us destroys the death in us, that we who were dead are alive again, we who were lost have been found. We are now free: free to forgive others, free to forgive ourselves, free to accept God's forgiveness. How can we be less human than God?

Oh yes, it calls for constant conversion, a ceaseless turning to God, an endless cry for forgiveness. We must root out the sins that violate the image of God in our brothers and sisters; above all, we must weed out those "sins of omission" where we do violence by doing nothing. But even here, in your continuing conversion, you are not left to yourself; your Father runs to meet you. Remember St. Augustine: "If we but turn to God, that itself is a gift of God."

It's so strange: The elder brother, the son who never sinned, turns out to be the servant, the slave—enslaved to his friend's commands, to his self-image, to his righteousness. Service has not freed him for love, for forgiveness. The prodigal has cast off his enslavement, the "loose living" (Lk 15:13) that bound him fast. He is free: free to beg "Forgive me," free to accept forgiveness, free to be son again, free to party in thanksgiving and joy. And the good, obedient, faithful son remains outside—angry, frustrated, unhappy.

Today, Laetare Sunday, Sunday of joy and rejoicing, you can take your pick. You can stay outside, aloof from the party, enjoying your anger, reveling in your wretchedness, refusing to forgive or be forgiven. Or you can let go of yesterday's death, join the party, celebrate God, celebrate yourself, celebrate your brothers and sisters, celebrate . . . life!

Dahlgren Chapel
Georgetown University
March 16, 1980

7
WHERE IS YOUR GOOD FRIDAY?
Good Friday

- *Isaiah 52:13—53:12*
- *Hebrews 4:4–16; 5:7–9*
- *John 18:1—19:42*

Today, my friends, the chips are down. On Good Friday you cannot avoid the Christian issue. At Christmas you can dream—of angels and a star, of a teen-age mother and an infant in straw. On Easter Sunday you will be glad and rejoice, because God and goodness have risen from the grave. But today there is no dreaming, today little rejoicing. Today you come face to face with the primary Christian symbol, and that symbol is . . . a cross. So, let's look briefly at some facts, and then ask what those facts say to us.

I

We begin with five facts. First, God died. On that drab afternoon 1,950 years ago, your God and mine died. Oh I know, death could not destroy divinity; the Trinity was not suddenly two persons. And still it is true: God died. On Calvary's cross there was only one person, and He was God. And He died. If there is one mystery harder to accept than "God was born," it is the mystery "God died." No wonder Patriarch Nestorius protested in the fifth century: "A born God, a dead God, a buried God I cannot adore."[1] In the sixties we were shocked by a theology that proclaimed God dead. You would have been shocked even more rudely on Calvary: God did indeed die.[2]

Second fact: Jesus really suffered. Don't fictionize Calvary. Don't imagine that, because Jesus was God, he felt pain less than we do. If anything, he suffered more intensely, he was more sensitive, alive to everything human. The crown on his head was plaited of real thorns; it was warm spit that spattered his face; a tough whip made his back flinch; those were sharp nails that pierced his hands and feet; the blood reddening Calvary's earth was his. "Into your hands I commit my spirit" was really his last breath. Little wonder he called out in the garden: "Father, take this cup away from me!" God, don't let me die!

Third fact: Jesus suffered and died for us. There are two protagonists in that passion: Jesus is one; the other is I. It is St. Paul's unbelieving whisper: "The Son of God . . . gave Himself *for me*" (Gal 2:20). He did not die for a misty mass called humanity. He died for Adam, that strange creature who could not abide in God's love for the space of one temptation. He died for Judas as well as for John, for Mary of Magdala as well as Mary of Nazareth. He died for *both* thieves who were crucified with him, even for the bandit who kept cursing him. He died for me, as if Christ and his cross had arms only for me. He died for every sinner and every sin from the first Eden till his final coming.

Fourth fact: Jesus died for me because he loved me. He did not have to die, did not die because he had no other choice: "No one takes [my life] from me; I lay it down of my own free will" (Jn 10:18). St. Paul has no doubt about the reason why: "the Son of God . . . loved me" (Gal 2:20). It's so difficult to accept—that God should die for love of me. It recalls Francis Thompson's "Hound of Heaven":

> "Strange, piteous, futile thing!
> Wherefore should any set thee love apart?
>   . . . Thou knowest not
> How little worthy of any love thou art!
> Whom wilt thou find to love ignoble thee
>   Save Me, save only Me?"³

Fifth fact: By his death Jesus gave me life. I am not denying that his whole life is life-giving; I am stressing the centerpiece of salvation's drama. Without his death I would be dead; I mean, I would be without faith, without hope, without love. Yes, without joy.

II

But what do these facts say to us? God died . . . a painful death . . . for me . . . out of love . . . to give me life. Therefore what? Therefore not only the ecstatic joy of human and Christian living; therefore the cross! Not outside Jerusalem; here and now. Not now and then; always. The words of Jesus are raw, rough, uncompromising: If you want to follow him, if you would be his disciple, you take up your cross daily (Lk 9:23). If you want to save your life, you must lose it . . . for Christ's sake (v. 24).

The point is: Salvation is indeed God's free gift, but it is not automatic. The cross of Christ has to be touched to me personally, individually. It is touched to me in several ways: through the death that is baptism; through the Eucharist that recaptures the death of Christ till he comes; but in a special way through my own cross, without which I cannot be his disciple. Like the life of Christ, my own life has to be a ceaseless dying-rising. I am indeed risen with Christ, but the paradox of Christian living is that I am not fully risen in this life. Christian living is a ceaseless movement to life through death—everyday death.

The problem is, what does it mean? What is this cross you must take up daily? It's easy enough to find the cross elsewhere: in the poverty of Appalachia, on the streets of Calcutta, in Cambodian refugee camps, in the apartheid of South Africa, in the hungers of Latin America, in Afghanistan's new graves, in the political prisons of Russia and the Philippines, in the American Embassy in Iran. It isn't hard to discover the cross in D.C. slums, in the schizophrenics at St. Elizabeth's. But where is *your* sharing in the passion of Christ?

I'm afraid I cannot tell you. You are, each of you, a unique authority on your Calvary. I dare not lay a cross on you; I can only provoke you into thinking. What do you usually avoid? And whom? Are you built only for comfort? Do you ever fast except to lose weight? . . . What keeps you from being a saint—from being like St. Paul, Mother Teresa, Jesus? Who matters most in your life? If you had to confess what you want out of human living, would it have anything to do with a crucified Lord? Where does he rank in your Top Ten? . . . How do you handle illness, from a common cold to the threat of cancer? What are you afraid of? Death? Life? . . . In whom do you see Christ? Only in those you like and who like you?

To whom do you give bread and drink? To the hungry and thirsty, or to the well-fed and well-oiled? When did you last welcome a stranger or give clothes to the naked? Who are the sick you visit? What prisons, of body or mind, have seen your face?

On this Good Friday, at this point in your existence, whom are you like? Mary? John? Pilate? Herod? Joseph of Arimathea? Peter? The disciples looking on from a safe distance?

The Church will survive heresy and hatred, sin and persecution. What imperils Catholicism is our lukewarmness: Jesus Christ does not turn us on. A rock group descends on Cincinnati and people stampede to their death. The Redskins miss the playoffs and the Potomac floods with our weeping. Bo Derek shows her "ten" and men slobber like crazy. But God dies on a cross for us and business goes on as usual; we keep tossing Frisbees at 3 p.m.

I am not asking for ceaseless emotion—wailing and weeping, or balloons and guitars. Emotion peters out. I am asking you to live your Christian commitment, to live day after day the dying-rising that Holy Week symbolizes. It is not enough to re-present the crucifixion of Christ liturgically, play it out once a year. The liturgy expresses ritually what goes on in the rest of our lives; the liturgical journey ritualizes the human journey. But does it? Does this afternoon's crucifixion sacramentalize what goes on in the rest of your life?

I've just read a remarkable book. Its title: *The Voice of Blood*.[4] It tells of five Jesuits. Ordinary people, ordinary talents, ordinary defects. One doubted for years that he was worth anything. One was tough for others to clue into. One was awfully distant, lived like Alice in Wonderland. One was something of a disaster as vice provincial and master of novices. One talked so much that they said you had to "subtract eleven and divide by two." They found Christ and his cross in El Salvador, in Rhodesia, in Brazil. Each found his dying-and-rising in service—to the poor and illiterate, in the bush, among teen-agers or Indians. Four years ago, each found his Good Friday; four years ago, each was murdered.

Where, my friends, where is *your* Good Friday?

Dahlgren Chapel
Georgetown University
April 4, 1980

EASTER

CHRIST IS ALIVE

LOVE PEACE LIVE LIFE LOVE PEACE LIFE LIVE PEACE ALIVE ∷

8
DO YOU LOVE ME?
Third Sunday of Easter (C)

- *Acts 5:27–32, 40–41*
- *Revelation 5:11–14*
- *John 21:1–9*

It should come as no surprise to you that today's lovely liturgy of love turns us in three directions. Each has to do with an apostle— an apostle in love. There is the prince of apostles; there is the lady apostle we celebrate today;[1] and there is the apostle that is you. A word on each.

I

First, the prince of apostles. Three facets of Peter's life emerge from today's Gospel: his rehabilitation, his commission, his destiny.[2]

Peter's rehabilitation. Today's Gospel scene goes back to a prediction and a fact. A prediction. At the Last Supper or on the way to the Mount of Olives, Jesus warned his disciples that they would fall away and be scattered, warned Peter that Satan would shake him, told Peter he could not follow his Master now.[3] Peter took issue with Jesus. Even if all others fell away, he would not; to follow Jesus, he was ready for prison and death. Jesus predicted that before the cock crowed, Peter would deny him thrice. Peter responded: I will die rather than deny. The fact? While Jesus was moving through his passion, Peter denied him three times. Denied he had been with Jesus in the garden, denied he was one of his disciples, denied he knew Jesus—denied it with curses and an oath.

The cock crowed; Jesus looked at Peter; Peter remembered what the Lord had said; and Peter wept bitterly.[4]

But in a touching scene Peter is rehabilitated, restored. The triple denial, "I don't know the man," is symbolically undone by Jesus' thrice-repeated "Do you love me?" and Peter's threefold "You know I love you." He is once again the disciple he denied being; he feels the love that makes for discipleship. His repentance is obvious. He insists passionately that he does indeed love; he is hurt that Jesus asks three times. Unlike the earlier Peter, he will not boast that he loves more than others; he simply asks Jesus to read his heart: "Lord, you know everything; you know well that I love you" (Jn 21:17).

The rehabilitation leads to a commission. Peter is sent (that is what "apostle" means), sent on mission, to feed Christ's flock. Not because he is worthy; why, he has denied the Master with an oath! He is chosen because God works through "the weak things of the world to shame the strong" (1 Cor 1:27). If there is a special authority here—to lead, teach, correct—it is not on power that the stress falls. The stress is on service, the service stressed in the first Letter of Peter: "Tend the flock of God that is in your care, exercising your role of overseer not by constraint but willingly, as God would have it, not for base gain but eagerly, not as domineering over those in your charge but by being examples to the flock" (1 Pet 5:2–3). Peter's model is the Good Shepherd of John's Gospel: He calls his sheep by name, goes before them, lays down his life for them (Jn 10:1–18).

The shepherd lays down his life. Yes, here is *Peter's* destiny too: The commission leads to a cross. "Truly, I assure you, when you were a young man, you used to fasten your own belt and set off for wherever you wished. But when you grow old, you will stretch out your hands, and another will fasten a belt around you and take you where you do not wish to go" (Jn 21:18). Jesus proclaims to Peter what his life of loving shepherding holds for him. He will die a bloody death; in fact, he will stretch out his hands on a cross, after the manner of his Master.[5] From conversion to commission to crucifixion—here is life and death for the prince of the apostles.

II

Second, the liturgy turns us to the lady apostle we celebrate today. The parallels to Peter are striking. I am not suggesting that

Mary Himens ever swore "I don't know the man." Fortunately for me, that is not essential to the parallelism. Still, twenty-five years ago she experienced a conversion, a turning to Christ. Our Lord asked her a probing question: "Mary Kathryn, do you love me more than these?" Like Peter, she did not answer the question fully. She did not know how much she loved him; even if she knew, she would not have weighed her love against her sisters in Christ. She simply murmured: "Lord, you know everything; you know well that I love you." And in witness to her love, she offered him three gifts: not gold, frankincense, and myrrh, but poverty, chastity, and obedience. She offered him . . . herself.

Three perilous gifts. For they involve a radical risk. She risked not becoming a woman.[6] By these three vows she risked declining the encounter with three elemental forces: the earth, man, and her own spirit. By the vow of poverty, she risked declining responsibility for her own livelihood, living off the community; she risked remaining irresponsible. By the vow of chastity, she risked refusing to enter the world of Adam, risked a premature senility (sex is dead), thinking herself whole when she was not. By the vow of obedience, she risked declining the most bruising encounter of all, the encounter with her own spirit and its power of choice. She risked being other-directed, with her choices made for her, refusing ultimate responsibility for them. She risked an end to aspiration and conflict; she could spare herself the lonely agony of the desert struggle.

She took the triple risk, in the conviction that God was calling and that God's grace could make her womanhood fruitful. From that conversion, from that turning to Christ, came a commission: "Feed my sheep." The sheep have been a motley flock—all shapes and sizes and colors, but with a special tenderness for the young— rams and ewes. Over these she has no power—save the irresistible force of love. To these her life sings the poetry of her beloved Gerard Manley Hopkins: "The world is charged with the grandeur of God." And even if

> . . . all is seared with trade; bleared, smeared with toil;
> and wears man's smudge and shares man's smell . . .
> . . . for all this, nature is never spent;
> There lives the dearest freshness deep down things . . .
> Because the Holy Ghost over the bent
> World broods with warm breast and with ah! Bring wings.[7]

Her power, she confesses, is the dynamism of the Spirit, who gives great joy to her soul, who through all her vowed risk has been fashioning a real, pulsing woman in the image of her who first whispered to God "Behold the bondmaid of the Lord; let it be to me according to your word" (Lk 1:38). Like Mary Magdalene, sent to the disciples by the risen Jesus, she proclaims to a fearful, tear-stained world: "I have seen the Lord" (Jn 20:18).[8]

As with Peter, so with Mary: The commission is linked to a cross. Not a final killing Calvary, though that too may be in the offing. Rather a thorn in the flesh decades-old. She experiences in her body a form of dying by which she glorifies God. It is a ceaseless share in Christ's passion that compels her to cry out with St. Paul: "I rejoice in my sufferings for your sake, and in my flesh I complete what is lacking in Christ's afflictions for the sake of his body . . . the Church" (Col 1:24). Like Peter, she has wept bitterly. Conversion, commission, crucifixion—here is life and death for our lady apostle.

III

Third, what of you? After all, this is not a cram course in John; it is not the canonization of a nun. Peter and Mary say something to us.

Know it or not, like it or not, conversion, commission, and crucifixion initiated your Christian existence. In your baptism you died to sin and self, you rose to God. Remember St. Paul's reminder to the Christians of Rome: "Do you not know that all of us who have been baptized into Christ Jesus were baptized into his death? We were buried therefore with him by baptism into death, so that as Christ was raised from the dead by the glory of the Father, we too might walk in newness of life" (Rom 6:3–4). Newness of life. At that moment Christ our Lord turned you to him *and* turned you to the world. Your baptismal conversion was your Christian commission to live the gospel in its crucifying fulness, to bring that gospel to flame in some small acre of God's world. In baptism you were commissioned an apostle; you were sent.

My problem is not with your baptism. If enough water flowed over you and the formula was trinitarian, the baptism was valid; it "took," however loud you screamed in protest. My problem is with the years that have fled since then. If you want to uncover how Christian your existence has been, consult the three c's: conversion, commission, crucifixion.

Has your life since baptism been a constant conversion, a ceaseless turning to Christ? I am not suggesting that you have turned totally from him, that you are in a state of serious sin. Quite the contrary. My experience of Christians is very much my experience of myself. If Jesus Christ were to ask me: "Walter, do you love me?", I would respond: "Lord, you know everything; you know well that I love you." But I rarely live the logic of that love. So much of my life is superficial. I mean, so many of my human acts are not fully human, do not engage me as a total person. They do not enslave me to Satan, but neither do they commit me to Christ. The danger in such semi-Christian living was strongly stated in the last book of the Bible, where Christ warns a congregation of Christians: "I know your works: you are neither cold nor hot. Would that you were cold or hot! So, because you are lukewarm, and neither cold nor hot, I will vomit you out of my mouth" (Rev 3:15–16).

And what of that baptismal commission? All too many Catholics have pigeonholed their apostolate, shelved it indefinitely. Or they leave it to professionals, like priests, or to missionaries, like Mother Teresa. No, my friends; each of you is on mission. From this draft there are no exemptions—not because you are in college or a demanding job, not because you are nearsighted or slow-witted, not because you are under 18 or over 45. You can indeed dodge this draft, but then you are unchristian; for a Sunday Christian is a contradiction. If you love me, Jesus insisted, you will keep my commandments (Jn 14:21). And he commands you not only to avoid adultery, but "Let your light so shine before men and women that they may see your good works and give glory to your Father who is in heaven" (Mt 5:16). If you are not bringing Christ anywhere, to anyone, then if Jesus asks you "Do you love me?", it might be more honest to reply "No, Lord, not really."

Of the third c, crucifixion, I need say little. The cross is inescapable, from the acne on an adolescent's cheek to the dying that rends flesh from spirit. You alone really know what nails crucify you. The question is, what do you do when "another fastens a belt around you and takes you where you do not wish to go" (cf. Jn

21:18)? Does the folly of *your* cross make any sense to you? Have you yet accepted the crucial Christian truth, that salvation comes through crucifixion—yours as well as Christ's?

Dear friends, my questions are not accusations. Within Catholicism I experience a community of love. That love is transparent right here. But the response of Peter and the jubilee of Mary raise an agonizing issue. If we Catholics are what we say we are, if we are turned in crucified love to Christ and his flock, why is the world we inhabit largely a jungle? Why is the District of Columbia a microcosm of hurt and hate, of injustice and oppression, of loneliness and lovelessness? Is our very mission a "mission impossible"? Or must we not pause before we echo Peter's last two words: "Lord, you know everything; [and so] you know that I . . ." what?

Dahlgren Chapel
Georgetown University
April 20, 1980

9
THAT THEY MAY HAVE LIFE
Fourth Sunday of Easter (A)

- *Acts 2:14, 36–41*
- *1 Peter 2:20–25*
- *John 10:1–10*

The heart of my homily is the last sentence in today's Gospel: "I came that they may have life, and have it in all its fulness" (Jn 10:10). I focus on life because no other word is more expressive of Easter. And I focus on life because the Gospel of John has been called the Gospel of life. Not only is life a favorite word in John. The author makes clear that this is why he wrote the Gospel: "that you may believe that Jesus is the Christ, the Son of God, and that believing you may have life in his name" (Jn 20:31). That you may have life.

No apologies, then, for preaching life. The problem is, how reveal its richness? How help you thrill, as John thrilled, to the life that is actually in you? Three questions may do it. First, what does being alive say to you? Second, what does it mean to be alive in Christ? Third, how alive are you?

I

First then, what does being alive say to you? This is important. John did not select "life" out of a hat; he selected it because it says something, because it is a powerful everyday symbol. It says different things to different people at different times. Martin Luther King crying "Free at last!" . . . Lazarus emerging from the tomb . . . astronauts walking on the moon . . . Pavarotti reaching his high C

65

... Alexander Fleming discovering penicillin ... a child licking a chocolate ice-cream cone. Each of these is thrillingly alive.

Recently I read a moving account of the cellist Pablo Casals. At ninety, he was dreadfully afflicted by rheumatoid arthritis and emphysema. Each morning was agony. He could hardly dress himself. He would shuffle into the living room each morning on the arm of his lovely young wife Marta, badly stooped, head pitched forward. He would move to the piano, arrange himself with difficulty on the bench, somehow raise his swollen, clenched fingers above the keyboard. Let Norman Cousins tell you what he saw:

> I was not prepared for the miracle that was about to happen. The fingers slowly unlocked and reached toward the keys like the buds of a plant toward the sunlight. His back straightened. He seemed to breathe more freely. Now his fingers settled on the keys. Then came the opening bars of Bach's [*Well-tempered Clavichord*], played with great sensitivity and control. . . . He hummed as he played, then said that Bach spoke to him here— and he placed his hand over his heart.
>
> Then he plunged into a Brahms concerto and his fingers, now agile and powerful, raced across the keyboard with dazzling speed. His entire body seemed fused with the music; it was no longer stiff and shrunken but supple and graceful and completely freed of its arthritic coils.
>
> Having finished the piece, he stood up by himself, far straighter and taller than when he had come into the room. He walked to the breakfast table with no trace of a shuffle, ate heartily, talked animatedly, finished the meal, then went for a walk on the beach.[1]

When have *you* felt gloriously alive, so brimful of life that it almost hurts? When you felt the first stirrings of another life within you or smiled for the first time on your newborn child? Skimming over a lake on skis, with the wind and the foam on your face? When someone's eyes met yours in ecstatic love? Touching the stars with your dance? Stuffing a basket high above the rim? Singing with abandon "The heavens are telling the glory of God"? Downing a mug of Michelob on a steamy hot day? When life sprang from your pen or your brush, from lifeless clay? When your healing hands touched life to weary flesh?

I remember a hushed midnight in Arizona, five thousand feet above sea level, a sky studded with stars. I feel a lifeless loaf break into the Bread of Life within my fingers. I look into your eyes and it "makes my spirit spin, my bones to quake, my blood run thin, my flesh to melt inside my skin, my very pulse create a din."[2] Neurotic, I sleep as little as I can, for sleep is too much like death, I hate to miss anything of life, and each hour trembles with fresh promise.

What makes *you* feel alive?

II

Which brings me to my second question: What does it mean to be alive in Christ? All the above—but raised to the nth power, lifted above anything the eye can see, the ear hear, our minds imagine. You see, when John speaks of "eternal life," he does not mean simply a life in a distant age, life in a heaven to come.[3] Eternal life is now. For eternal life is, to begin with, the life by which God Himself lives, the life the Son of God possesses from the Father (Jn 5:26; 6:57). To give this life to us, God's Son took flesh from us. You remember how John's First Letter opens: "That which was from the beginning, which we have heard, which we have seen with our eyes, which we have looked upon and touched with our hands, concerning the word of life [Christ]—the life was made manifest, and we saw it, and testify to it, and proclaim to you the eternal life which was with the Father and was made manifest to us" (1 Jn 1:1–2). Not only are Jesus' words life-giving (Jn 6:63); Jesus is our life (11:25; 14:6).

How can we receive that life? Only, John tells us, only by believing in Jesus. How is eternal life communicated to us? As natural life was given when God breathed His breath, His spirit, into the dust of the earth (Gen 2:7), so eternal life is given when Jesus breathes forth God's Holy Spirit upon the disciples (Jn 20:22). The Holy Spirit is the life-giving force (Jn 6:63), the Spirit given after Jesus has conquered death (7:39). Through the ages the Spirit is given through the living waters of baptism that beget a man or woman anew (3:5; 4:10; 7:37–39). And this eternal life is nourished by the body and blood of Jesus in the Eucharist (6:51–58).

It is an incredible truth, an exciting exchange: When Jesus took our humanity, he made it possible for us to share his divinity. Eternal life is not poetic fancy. "Eternal life," Jesus said to his Father the night before he was to die, "consists in this, that they know you, the only true God, and the one whom you sent, Jesus Christ"

(Jn 17:3). This is not some abstract knowledge, some intellectual understanding a theologian might uncover, knowing *about* God from reason or revelation. Here, to "know" is to share by faith a living, intimate relationship with the Father and Jesus.

Your living oneness with a living Trinity is so real and so mystery-laden that the New Testament resorts to striking symbols, strong metaphors, to suggest how close it is. Jesus is the vine, you are the branches that live from that vine (Jn 15:1 ff.). You are a dwelling place, and Father and Son make their home within you (Jn 14:23). You are a temple, and God's Spirit dwells in you (1 Cor 3:16–17).

So strong, so enduring, so eternal is this life that even death cannot destroy it. "Whoever feeds on this bread," Jesus declared, whoever feeds on his flesh given for the life of the world, "will live forever" (Jn 6:51). Oh yes, you will die the death of the flesh. But despite that terrible wrenching of soul from body, despite that fearful movement into apparent darkness, you whose life in Christ is nourished by his sacramental body and blood will continue to live that life beyond the grave. You will never cease to be branches on the vine that is Christ, temples of the Spirit, dwelling places of God One and Three.

III

You are indeed living shrines of God. But the most difficult question remains: How alive are you? We all know people who, while not dead, are only half alive. The Nazi Rudolf Hess, now in his eighties, "living" out his fourth decade in a German jail. Workers on an assembly line, doing the same monotonous thing over and over again. Students putting in time until they graduate, until they get into the "real" world. Two people "living" out their marriage together, but in dull routine, in a rut.

Similarly for the life of the spirit, for life in Christ. What agonizes me is the large number of Christians who have God's life in them but are barely alive. They do everything they have to do, stay out of serious sin, have little if anything to confess. But the Christ within them does not thrill them, gives them fewer goose-pimples than Starsky and Hutch. Jesus' death bothers them less than John Lennon's. They look for something else to "turn them on": yoga, rock 'n' roll, the Redskins, a kibbutz in Israel, Star Wars, Lawrence

Welk. And so many Christians are in despair because they lack some essential ingredient of contemporary commercial existence, from hair curled with Clairol to a body free of human smell.

But why? Dear God, why? We are Christophers, Christ-bearers, whether we are a "ten" or a "minus two." Deep within us runs the life of God, like another bloodstream. We are risen with Christ, our sins have been forgiven us, we can call God Father. Whenever we wish it, we can feed on the flesh of Christ, get intoxicated on his blood. His word resounds, he himself transpires, in our coming together. We are "a chosen race, a royal priesthood, a holy nation, God's own people" (1 Pet 2:9). It is enough to make us leap for joy, like John the Baptist in Elizabeth's womb.

In Elizabeth's womb. . . . It brings us back, this Mother's Day, to life at its source. Here, on a natural level, is the closest resemblance to the Christlife we live. Recall the moving cry of St. Paul to the Galatians: "My little children, with whom I am again in travail until Christ be formed in you!" (Gal 4:19). Life in Christ is Christ in us—Christ growing in us until he reaches in us the full measure of his humanity, until we become fully human, fully alive.

To be aware of Jesus' life stirring within you, as a mother is sensitive to the fetal life shaping in her flesh, this is Easter existence. Is it your existence? Not knowing it abstractly, but feeling it in your bones? At times thrilling to it, as you thrill to surf and sand and sky, to Leonard Bernstein or Bruce Springsteen, to the touch of love? As Mary thrilled to the touch of Christ within her?

The paradox is, life can be full and still be spotted with pain. The proof stares you in the face, from Christ to Casals, from the mother of Jesus to every mother among you. But to live Christ's passion with Easter joy,. it is not enough to *have* life, even God's life. You must *live* life, feel it, open up to it, let it sway you and have its way with you. Life's real enemy is not pain, not even death; life's enemy is boredom.

My friends, I recommend to you my own Easter prayer: "Lord, let me never get bored!"

Dahlgren Chapel
Georgetown University
May 10, 1981

10
LIVE ON IN ME
Fifth Sunday of Easter (B)

- *Acts 9:26–31*
- *1 John 3:18–24*
- *John 15:1–8*

Today's Gospel stresses a thrilling theme. In his farewell discourse, in his last will and testament, Jesus commands the Eleven: "Remain in me as I remain in you" (Jn 15:4a). Live on in me as I live on in you. This, for John, is a precious expression, a favorite expression. It expresses a communion—a personal communion, an inward communion, an enduring communion.[1] I want to explore that communion on three levels. I want to move from the month of May to Mother's Day to every day. Because this is the month of May, I shall touch that expression, "Remain (live on) in me as I remain (live on) in you," to the relationship between Mary and Jesus. Because this is Mother's Day, I shall link it to the communion between every mother and the child of her womb. And because we are a Christian community, I shall apply it to the profound oneness between each one of us and the Christ who is our life.

I

First then, Mary and Jesus. There is a special sense, a unique sense, in which Jesus could have said to Mary "Live on in me as I live on in you." One of the most mind-shattering of Christian mysteries is enshrined in the single word "Incarnation." For nine months God's own Son remained, lived on, within the body of a teen-age Jewish girl. He took flesh of her flesh, lived in her as truly

70

as I lived inside my own mother, was fed by her blood and kept alive in her. Mary's life was Jesus' life; without her, outside of her, he would have died. He lived literally in and off her body, in and off her life.

But, as St. Augustine pointed out centuries ago, simply conceiving Christ in her flesh would hardly have profited Mary. A miracle indeed—enough to make headlines till his second coming. But the Incarnation as a physical fact tells us little about the mother of Jesus. That is why Augustine insisted: "Mary was more blessed because she laid hold of faith in Christ than because she conceived the flesh of Christ. . . . Her motherly relationship to him would have been of no use to Mary had she not carried Christ in her heart more happily even than she carried him in her womb." She "conceived Christ in her mind before she conceived him in her womb." "It was by faith she gave him birth, it was by faith she conceived him."[2]

A remarkable insight, a bold remark: It was by faith that Mary conceived her child, it was by faith that she gave birth to him. Jesus lived in her, in her flesh as well as her spirit, because she believed. I am not saying that Mary knew from the beginning, at the dawn of the Incarnation, the full mystery of God-with-us; what God revealed to her is largely hidden from our eyes, and the Gospel story makes clear that the mother of Jesus had to grow in understanding, even of her own child. But is it credible that the Son of God would have taken flesh of a teen-age girl, would have made his home within her body, not of a human father but of the Holy Spirit, if God had not disclosed to her something of the miracle of this unique conception, if God had not asked for her free, faith-filled yes? In some way she had to say "I believe, Lord, help my unbelief." The early Church was convinced of this. Remember how Luke has Mary responding to God's messenger "Be it done unto me according to thy word" (Lk 1:38)? Remember how Luke has her cousin Elizabeth, mother of John the Baptist, crying out that Mary is blessed because she "believed that what was spoken to her from the Lord would be fulfilled" (Lk 1:45)?

Because Mary believed, not only did Jesus live in her; she lived in him. Not only did she share her life with him; he shared his life with her, the life of the God-man, like another bloodstream. And as she grew in loving faith, she grew in life—in the life that is Christ. Now, and endlessly, she lives in him as he lives in her.

II

My second point: every loving mother and the child of her womb. Here the words "Live on in me as I live on in you" resonate richly. So much could be said, so much ought to be said; but time is our enemy. Let me touch those biblical words briefly to only two facets of that extraordinarily personal, inward, enduring communion. Do forgive me if I speak now in the first person; for once, the ego will not be selfish—and, who knows, I may even speak to your own experience!

The first facet focuses on nine hidden months. The first person I ever touched was the mother in whom I lived; and I am grateful for the life she fed me in our touching. But more impressive to me in recent years is a truth which the psychiatrist Karl Stern brought home to me.[3] Those nine months are the natural foundation for a type of knowing that surpasses all others: I mean knowledge by being, knowledge through union, knowledge through love.

You see, all my knowing is woefully weak, dreadfully inadequate, as long as what I know, or even the person I know, is merely an object, stands over against me, outside of me. The most perfect form of knowledge is not a mathematical equation, a foolproof argument, an accumulation of facts. Knowing is most perfect where knower and known are fused into one. Here is where knowledge becomes love. If anything makes me humble in the pride of all my heaped-up knowledge, it is the fact that the model of human knowing is to be found in my mother: She knew by being, she knew in loving, she knew me (and so much else) by being one with me in the most intimate union this world knows: I in her, and she in me. That is the kind of knowing which will find ultimate perfection when I am one with God in beatifying vision.

The second facet focuses on my mother's total mothering. My "earliest love story" is "strangely intermingled with a story of severing, of gently pushing away, of farewell."[4] That final, triumphant thrust that launched me into an unsuspecting world, that severed umbilical cord, these were only the beginnings, the symbols, of a love bent on liberating, bent on gradually freeing me from bondage to her, so as to live my own life, to be open to others, open to loving and sharing. Even when I left home for good, at the ripe age of sixteen and a half, I can remember only her sweet, encouraging smile; I was not allowed to see the tears.

The result? A glorious paradox. My mother has lived on in me more richly than if she had clutched me desperately. Conversely, because she turned my face towards others, I lived on in her more fully than if she had fixed my gaze on her alone. "Live on in me as I live on in you." It is possible only if you are willing to let go.

III

My third point: How does that expression, "Remain (live on) in me as I remain (live on) in you," touch the profound oneness between each one of us and the Christ who is our life? The fact is, the command of Christ has to do precisely with that communion; for it sums up our life of grace, a mystery-laden intimacy that raises us to a new level of existence. Let me explain.

The life you live as a Christian is not ordinary human existence simply stimulated by the example of Christ. By your baptism you are what St. Paul called "a new creation" (2 Cor 5:17). Why? Because you are "in Christ." And so you not merely *do* different things, like eating the body of Christ. You not merely do things differently, like giving a poor fellow a cup of cold water in the name of Christ. No, you *are* different.

But what does it mean to be "in Christ"? What is it that makes you different? That is what today's Gospel is all about. Jesus tells us what it means in striking imagery: "I am the vine; you are the branches" (Jn 15:5). The stress here is on life, divine life. As the vine in a vineyard gives its life to the branches, in somewhat the same way "the real vine" (v. 1), Christ our Lord, shares his life with those who are linked to him. As long as you remain in him through loving faith, he remains in you through faithful love; you live his life; you are Christ.

It is a relationship that alters you radically, transforms you. Catholicism cries out against those who claim that the movement from sin to grace does not really change you, that you are justified in that God by some legal make-believe attributes to you the justice of Christ, that your sins are not really blotted out but only covered over by the merits of our Savior. No, you are indeed a new creation; for God gives Himself to you, is present to you in a new way, makes it possible for you to know and love Him in a manner impossible to your naked nature.

How important is it that you live in Christ, and Christ in you? Listen to him: "Apart from me you can do nothing" (v. 5). Nothing? We theologians have debated that hard saying for centuries; this is not the place to rehearse those debates. But this much can be said: If you are severed from "the real vine," you are spiritually dead. You are "like a branch, cast off and withered, which they collect and throw into the fire to be burned" (v. 6). And if you are dead, you cannot do the works of life, the works of Christ. Whatever "good" you may do, it will not lead you or anyone else to the life that is Christ. On the other hand, if you live in Christ and he lives in you, the fruit you can bear is beyond telling. In fact, you can "ask for whatever you want and it will be done for you" (v. 7).

To conclude, two quick observations. First, if you are anxious to know how real and how deep is your personal, inward, enduring communion with Jesus, simply ask yourself how real and how deep is your personal, inward, enduring communion with your brothers and sisters. For chapter 15 will continue with a divine command: "Love one another as I have loved you" (v. 12). If you do not bear that much fruit, you may well be dying on the vine.

A second observation. Some Scripture scholars argue—persuasively, I think—that the vine in this chapter has Eucharistic overtones.[5] In Johannine circles it served an exhortatory purpose: "insisting that eucharistic union must last and bear fruit and must deepen the union between Jesus and his disciples already existing through love."[6]

That secondary theme is splendidly appropriate today. In a few short moments a Georgetown student will receive his First Communion. For several years Chew Liung has been worshiping with you here at noon-ten. Last Thursday evening he was baptized and took the name Thomas. That ceremony sealed, in moving fashion, the faith and love that have marked his mind and heart for quite some time: He has long been living in Jesus, and Jesus in him. Today that personal, inward, enduring communion will deepen beyond measuring: He will pillow Christ on his tongue, cradle him in his flesh. As we share the joy that is his, may we thrill to the gift that is ours: God-with-us lives in us, and we live in him. For us, as for St. Paul, "to live is Christ" (Phil 1:21).

Dahlgren Chapel
Georgetown University
May 13, 1979

11
PEACE I LEAVE TO YOU
Sixth Sunday of Easter (C)

- *Acts 15:1–2, 22–29*
- *Revelation 21:10–14, 22–23*
- *John 14:23–29*

In our Catholic vocabulary we have a number of momentous monosyllables. Deceptively simple monosyllables. God, Christ, church; faith, hope, love; prayer, cross, hell. They leave our lips so easily, yet each is chock-full of meaning, of mystery.

Another of those monosyllables meets us in today's Gospel. During his last discourse Jesus tells his disciples: "Peace I leave to you" (Jn 14:27). Peace. What could be simpler? Any ninny knows what peace is. Actually, not simple at all—not the peace of Christ. And so, three questions: (1) Where is the problem with peace? (2) What does peace mean in the promise of Jesus? (3) What ought the word "peace" say to us?

I

First then, where is the problem with peace? The problem was put powerfully by Archbishop Thomas Becket. You may remember the Christmas sermon shaped for Becket by T. S. Eliot in *Murder in the Cathedral:* "Does it seem strange to you that the angels should have announced Peace, when ceaselessly the world has been stricken with War and the fear of War? Does it seem to you that the angelic voices were mistaken, and that the promise was a disappointment and a cheat?"[1]

The point is, the promise clashes with the reality. Not only for Becket, but for us too, there is no peace. Russia rapes Afghanistan; genocide decimates Cambodia; Christians murder one another in

75

the north of Ireland; a tenuous truce trembles over the Middle East and South Africa; atomic destruction threatens the whole race; our streets are avenues of war. Where do you spy peace on earth?

In fact, Scripture itself is a paradox; some would call it a flat contradiction. At his borning and his dying, Jesus promises peace. But in the midst of his preaching he warns: "Do not think I have come to bring peace on earth. I have not come to bring peace but a sword" (Mt 10:34), "dissension," division, disunity (Lk 12:51).

Is our liturgy, then, a make-believe, mere pretense? We run around hugging one another. "Peace!" we cry. "Shalom!" And there is no peace. Is peace really possible? Or is "peace" another of those weasel words that allow Christians to live at ease in a world at war, to forget that the real world is out there, and that world is fashioned of blood and tears? To forget that there is a real world inside ourselves, and that world too is at war, seethes with passions and fears, at times with anger and hate?

II

A genuine problem, I assure you. It raises a second question: What does peace mean in the promise of Jesus? For that, you must go back a moment to the Old Testament.[2] Biblical peace has so rich a content that no single English word can render it. It means that things are going well with you; you are happy; you feel secure; you have friends; you have a fruitful land, eat your fill and sleep without fear, multiply your progeny and triumph over your enemies.

But, for the Israelite, peace was not simply harmony with nature, with self, with others. True peace meant harmony with God, a right relationship with Yahweh; for "the Lord is peace" (Judg 6:24). In this sense peace was salvation, a salvation that was indeed being worked out in history but would be realized to perfection only in ultimate communion with Him who gives all that is good. Such is the meaning of Solomon's Wisdom: "The souls of the righteous are in the hand of God. . . . In the eyes of the foolish they seemed to have died . . . and their going from us [was thought] to be their destruction; but they are at peace" (3:1–3).

Precisely here is the bond between the Old Testament and the New. The peace Jesus announces is a saving peace. "*My* peace I give to you; not as the world gives do I give to you" (Jn 14:27).

Luke is so clear on this. The sinful woman who washed his feet
with her tears can "go in peace" because her sins have been forgiv-
en (Lk 7:50, 48). With their greeting "Peace to this house" (Lk
10:5), the disciples offer salvation to the towns where Jesus will
come. As they escort Jesus with joy into Jerusalem, their cry of
"peace" proclaims a redemption which the city will reject (Lk
19:38). And when they go out to radiate Easter peace to the ends
of the earth, Peter preaches: "You know the word which [God] sent
to Israel, preaching the good news that is peace through Jesus
Christ" (Acts 10:36–37). The gospel is peace, and peace is the gospel.

What Luke narrates, Paul explains. The heart of his message is
a short, glorious sentence: "He is our peace" (Eph 2:14). If you forget all else, remember that resounding affirmation: Christ is our
peace. How? Here Paul bursts the bonds of language; he is enraptured. Christ is our peace because he "has broken down the wall of
hostility" that divides Jew and Gentile, "that he might create in
himself one new man in place of the two, so making peace, and
might reconcile us both to God" (Eph 2:14–16). Christ is our peace
because "through him God was pleased to reconcile to Himself all
things . . . making peace by the blood of his cross" (Col 1:19–20).
Christ is our peace because only through him do all of us "have
access in one Spirit to the Father" (Eph 2:18). Christ is our peace
because it is by his gathering us "in a single body" that his peace
rules in our hearts (Col 3:15).

This is the peace that is "the fruit of the Spirit" (Gal 5:22), the
peace that "passes all understanding" (Phil 4:7), the peace that en-
dures in distress and tribulation (Rom 5:1–5), the peace that "will
keep your hearts and your minds in Christ Jesus" (Phil 4:7). This is
the peace that will find its consummation in endless, rapturous
communion with God. For the biblical "God of peace" is a God
who saves; and a heart at peace is a heart one with its God in
Christ.

III

If such is the gospel of peace, God's own good news, what
should the word "peace" say to us? In the first place, it should
challenge our Christian intelligence. What meaning above all others does "peace" have for you? It will vary, of course. For a soldier,
peace is the absence of war; for a politician, perhaps Salt II; for a

mother, a child asleep. If you live on campus, peace can be a silent stereo. Peace might be soft sand bathed in moonlight, the end of a tough day, the epilogue of love-making, the closing of class, feet up and a chilled Michelob. If you hurt, peace is an hour without pain.

Now each of these is indeed a facet of peace. But do you sense that the peace Christ left you is deeper than any of these, a peace the world cannot give, that it is the presence of God within you, all around you, a communion with Trinity that draws you into divine life, a sharing in the life of God's very own Son? At bottom, the peace of Christ is not a psychological state resulting from God's life within you; peace *is* your communion with God. You have been reconciled to Him through Christ; you are one with Him in love. Is this how you understand peace?

But if this is basic Christian peace, then the peace of Christ can coexist with war in the world, with human agony, with death and the myriad forms of human dying. This coexistence Christ predicted: "I have said this to you that in me you may find peace. In the world you find suffering, but have courage: I have conquered the world" (Jn 16:33). The "world" here is all that which is hostile to God, where sin tyrannizes, hate smothers love, death destroys life—humankind inasmuch as it is anti-God. In that world, where you must live and die, you will indeed find distress and tribulation. God never promised you a rose garden. In that world you indeed need courage to survive, to overcome; and your courage comes from the fact that Jesus Christ, who *is* your peace, has conquered the world, has broken its power, not by force but by a total surrender to love consummated in crucifixion.

But coexistence is not enough. It will not do to clutch the peace of Christ like Linus' blanket *and* endure the world's distress with a stiff upper lip. Precisely because you have been reconciled to God in Christ, precisely because the life of the risen Lord flows through you like another bloodstream, you have been sent, have been missioned, to this world at war, this world in distress. If Christ conquered the world, so must each Christian. This the exalted Christ tells us in the book called Revelation: "He who conquers, I will grant him to sit with me on my throne, as I myself conquered and sat down with my Father on His throne" (Rev 3:21). And, like Christ, you conquer the world not by force but by faith (1 Jn 5:4–5), a living faith, a loving faith—yes, a crucifying faith.

I am not asking you to drive Russia from Afghanistan; that is unreal. I *am* asking you: What wars have you ended in your back yard or your bedroom? What mines of envy or hate, of discord or dislike, have you defused on your corridor? Who hurts less because you love more? Who hurts more because you love less? Who was depressed but has come alive at your touch? Is anyone free to laugh because you have swallowed your pride? Who is hungry, for food or affection, and is fed by your faith? Who thirsts for justice and feels more human because you are there? Who experiences God's absence and finds the image of God on your face? My friends, this "world" of which John speaks is ultimately smallness and sin—and so we are part of the world that has to be overcome. You overcome it only as Jesus did: by touching to it the peace Christ has left to you, the communion with God that has made you a new creature.

The paradox is: By opening your heart to others you will *experience* the peace of Christ that is there, *feel* his real presence. Otherwise the peace of Christ may become a cold theological truth: He is our peace and he is within me. Away with cold theological truths! Do you want to feel the peace of Christ, glow with it? Then share it, give it away!

My brothers and sisters in Christ: In a few moments you will wish one another peace. I do not ask you to renounce whatever blessings peace means for you. By all means, wish one another freedom from war without and anxiety within; wish one another harmony and health; pray indeed that in every way they may fare well. But, over and above all these good things, realize what it is that a Christian nourished on Scripture wishes another Christian when you say "peace." With all my heart, I wish you, and pray for you, the salvation God took flesh to bring, the redemption from sin Christ bought with his blood. I wish you the grace of God that is the beginning of glory, that is eternal life here and now. I wish you deeper and deeper oneness with God. I pray that you will feel it, that the presence of Christ will make your "spirit spin," your "bones to quake," your "blood run thin," your "flesh to melt inside [your] skin," your "very pulse create a din"—aware "That Heaven is / Not *up*, but *in!*"[3]

Dahlgren Chapel
Georgetown University
May 11, 1980

Thanking

ORDINARY TIME

⸭

12
CALLED TO BE SAINTS
Second Sunday of the Year (A)

- *Isaiah 49:3, 5–6*
- *1 Corinthians 1:1–3*
- *John 1:29–34*

Last month the Kennedy Center for the Performing Arts honored five remarkable American artists. If you saw it, in person or on TV, you witnessed an "event." Not because "the beautiful people" were there. Not simply because it was splendidly staged. Rather for what it said about five people: conductor-composer Leonard Bernstein, choreographer Agnes de Mille, operatic singer Leontyne Price, actress Lynn Fontanne, and actor James Cagney.

These men and women had been called to greatness, and they had responded. Not halfheartedly, but with every fiber of their being. Not part time, but every waking moment. Not only in success and ecstasy, but through fire and cloud. The result? They have literally transformed our human living. Because of their artistry much of America is different. Through their genius we have experienced the human with new eyes, with fresh hearing. In their art we have touched the stars. We have felt more deeply, wept more bitterly, laughed more lustily, loved more passionately. Bernstein's *Mass* and *West Side Story,* de Mille's *Oklahoma* and *Rodeo,* Price's *Aïda,* Fontanne's *Pygmalion,* Cagney's *Yankee Doodle Dandy*—a thousand and one artistic miracles have lifted us out of ourselves, made us share fresh visions of the human, given us sights and sounds that transcend the humdrum, the ordinary, the muck and mire of our smallness. They were called to be artists; they became artists, great artists; and we . . . we are the richer for it, we come alive.

Dear brothers and sisters in Christ: You too have been called to greatness. You are "called to be saints" (1 Cor 1:2). The words are not mine; they stem from St. Paul. And Paul is merely rephrasing his Master: "You must be perfect as your heavenly Father is perfect" (Mt 5:48). Because sanctity is a vocation as sublime as Bernstein's, as soaring as Price's, as imaginative as de Mille's, as fetching as Fontanne's, as down-to-earth as Cagney's, I want to develop three ideas about it. First, what does it mean, "called to be saints"? Second, what does sanctity demand of you? Third, what will it do—for you and your world?

I

First, what does it mean, "called to be saints"? Isn't it a bit silly, or ambitious, or pretentious, or proud? Aren't "saints" very special people, a minority, an upper class, an unusual breed? Stephen stoned for Jesus' sake or Sebastian riddled with arrows, Antony in his wilderness or Simeon on his pillar, Benedict dotting the landscape with monasteries and Teresa with convents, Julian of Norwich enraptured in God and Francis Xavier capturing India for Christ—here is the stuff of sanctity! What does it have to do with us nice, ordinary people belting out hymns in Dahlgren and enjoying our Christian company?

Not much; just everything. Sanctity is your Christian calling. Simply because to be a saint, to be holy, is basically to be one with God. It means you live the two great commandments of the law and the gospel: Love God more than anything else, love your brothers and sisters at least as much as you love yourself. Do that and you are a saint. Oh, not heroic holiness, not yet love unto crucifixion—but essential sanctity. Without that much holiness, you are only nominally Christian, a Christian in name alone.

The marvel of it is, the power to do this, the capacity to be saints, you already have. God lives within you. His life courses through you like another bloodstream. You need not look around you; you need not search for a magic formula, feed questions into a giant computer. Your holiness is within you: Father, Son, and Holy Spirit at home in you. You *are* one with God. And so you are an incredible people, a royal priesthood, children of the Father, brothers and sisters of Christ, shrines of the Spirit. This is what lifts you out of yourself, out of your native smallness, makes you different, transforms you, gives you a fresh vision of what the human can be.

The point is, you not only *can* be holy. If God is tented in you, you *are* holy, you *are* a saint. You may not like the term, but you'd better get used to it. It's another word for Christian.

II

But sanctity is not a static state; oneness with God ought to be dynamic. And so my second question: What does holiness, being a saint, demand of you? The First Letter of John puts it succinctly: "By this we know that we are in [Jesus]: he who says he abides in [Jesus] ought to walk the way he walked" (1 Jn 2:5–6). *There* is the Christian's vocation to greatness—simple and awesome. To live holy lives, all you have to do is live like Jesus! I don't mean you have to imitate the raw details of his life—come to birth in a feeding trough, have no place whereon to lay your head, be betrayed by your best friends, die naked on a cross. What you must mirror, at all costs, is his love.

To do that, you have to love your Christian existence as deeply as Agnes, Lenny and Jimmy, Lynn and Leontyne loved their art. You won't make it if you sit still, if you cut corners, if you are content with a minimum, if you just avoid mortal sin, if you ask how much you *have* to do. You must love your oneness with Christ and his human images with a crucifying passion. This is what you want more than anything else in this world—more than money or music, success or sex, peace or power.

What will an artist do for art's sake? Starve, shiver with cold, forgo sleep, endure mental torture, skip normal pleasures, do the same blasted thing a thousand times, refuse to settle for second best. Because he or she is fashioning something extraordinary, something destined to endure, a work of strength or tenderness, of loveliness or sensitivity, a monument to human creativity, to man's quest for the spirit in the world. Only so do you end up with a *Giselle* or a *Pietà*, an *Iliad* or a *Messiah*, a *Brothers Karamazov* or a *Last Judgment*, a *Virgin Spring* or *A Man for All Seasons*—yes, even *I Wanna Hold Your Hand.*

And so with you and me. There is no way you and I may live Christianity part time, with half our hearts in it. I do not know what particular road God wants you to follow. The way of Dorothy Day,

Mother Teresa, Francis of Assisi, ordained priest need not be yours; but no matter. Lawyer or doctor, mother or father, student or teacher, typist or executive, healthy or infirm, young or middle-aged or old—whatever and wherever you are, you are called to live as Jesus lived. The call was born of your baptism, your mission to preach and live the gospel in your little acre.

It is indeed an art rather than a science. Your basic score is God's self-revealing in Christ. But that is not a lifeless book. You should be forever listening for fresh inspiration, and the primary Inspirer is the Holy Spirit—the Spirit who speaks within you, speaks in the images of Christ who surround you, speaks through the changing events of your history, speaks in the eloquence of things, from the tender tulip to our fearsome technology. With such inspiration you can shape and reshape your Christian being, write and rewrite the music of your life, dance daringly through the human comedy, play your varying roles on the stage of a constantly shifting world. It's the agony of the artist, ceaselessly creating, incessantly improving, endlessly dissatisfied, now and again in despair—because the Christ you are re-creating is always so near and yet so far, because in the presence of Love you are ever so far from Love. You are at once saint and sinner.

III

And what will all this do—for you and your world? I can promise you this: You will be ceaselessly surprised by the Spirit. Oh yes, you will burn, agonize, die a thousand deaths; you won't be canonized alive in Kennedy Center. But like every saint from Mother Mary to Mother Seton, like a host of unsung men and women who have lived the Christian life, you will know a profound peace. And there will be moments when you can scarcely contain yourself, when you will want to shout for joy, sing God's glory, "tell it on the mountain."

More importantly, you will change the little world you touch, even if it's just one man, one woman, one child. If a Picasso *Mother and Child,* a *pas de deux* by Fonteyn and Nureyev, a Pavarotti high C can move a human heart to rhapsody, what joy can you bring if you carry Christ all day, everywhere you go? You do it by being, by being who you are, by being Christlike. Paradoxically, not by natural gifts, not by vast knowledge or superstrength, not because you have the world by the tail. Rather the startling principle of St. Paul: "When I am weak, then I am strong" (2 Cor 12:10). The unique feature of your art, the art of being Christian, what makes your art different from Bernstein's or Cagney's, is that your strength lies in your weakness—if you will let your Lord take hold of you. For, as he said to Paul, "My grace is sufficient for you, for my power is made perfect in weakness" (2 Cor 12:9). Let Christ take hold of you and you will bring healing to the heavy-burdened. For to heal you need not be smart or muscular, you need not be a "ten," you do not need a flashing smile or bright blue eyes, a commanding presence or a resonant voice, the oils of ordination. You need only to love God and people with a consuming passion . . . and let yourself go!

Then your world will begin to change. Because of you, someone will experience the human with fresh eyes, will listen to Christ with ears open, will feel the touch of God, will find truth and beauty and goodness in a world that seemed desperately bleak and empty. Someone will discover *from you* that to be genuinely Catholic is to be alive with love and laughter. A man, a woman, a child will be less lonely, sense that someone cares, feel needed, wanted, loved.

Dear saints in Christ: Back in the fifth century, a splendid pope and preacher, Leo the Great, said in a Christmas sermon: "Christian, recognize your dignity!"[1] That command I echo today: Men and women of this Dahlgren community, recognize your dignity! God became what you are, that you might become what He is.[2] A God-man died for you, that you might live for God and man. God lives in you, that you might live in Him. Recognize that dignity and you will recognize your calling. Simply, be what you are. Saints, live like saints. Christ-bearers, act like Christ-bearers. You are called to greatness; then be great!

Dahlgren Chapel
Georgetown University
January 18, 1981

13
TO EACH IS GIVEN. . . .
Second Sunday of the Year (C)

- *Isaiah 62:1–5*
- *1 Corinthians 12:4–11*
- *John 2:1–12*

Over a hundred years ago, the adviser to Pius X on English affairs, Mgr. George Talbot, wrote a letter to the Archbishop of Westminster, Henry Manning. That letter, dated April 25, 1867, contained an important question and supplied a provocative reply. "What is the province of the laity? To hunt, to shoot, to entertain. These matters they understand, but to meddle with ecclesiastical affairs they have no right at all. . . ."[1]

I recalled that remarkable reply while mulling over St. Paul's remarks to the Christians of Corinth on "spiritual gifts" (1 Cor 12:1), "divine gifts," "charisms" (12:4). But if I found that nineteenth-century theology of the laity amusing, I am not at all amused by a twentieth-century parallel. In my experience, all too many Catholics feel that they have little or nothing to offer the Christian community, that the work of redemption has been farmed out to a small group of ordained men, that they themselves do not mediate God's grace and salvation, they merely receive it. The thesis not only smacks of heresy; more significantly, it spells the death of genuine spirituality and is destructive of Christian community.

A strong challenge to that false thesis is St. Paul's exciting sentence: "To each is given the manifestation of the Spirit for the common good" (1 Cor 12:7). That sentence enshrines three tremendous truths: (1) God's gifts are given to each of you. (2) These gifts stem from the Holy Spirit. (3) They are given to you for the good of all.

I

First then, each of you has spiritual gifts, divine gifts, gifts that minister to the community—the "in" word is charisms. In the reading from 1 Corinthians, Paul mentions a handful. Some Christians are gifted to present a message of wisdom; some expound effectively the truths of Christianity; some have the kind of faith that moves mountains; some bring healing to flesh or spirit, perform other miracles; some predict the future or move to repentance; some can tell who is guided by the Spirit and who is not; some speak in tongues, others translate what the tongues have to say.[2]

But these are illustrations, in the context of Corinthian concerns. The point I want to make is this: God gives His charisms to *all* Christians. You dare not restrict these gifts to exceptional children of God or to the structured Church, to saints or bishops, to Mother Teresa or the local clergy. Nor can you limit them to extraordinary gifts, to the miraculous, the sensational. The basic gifts God gives His people are given in baptism: the power to believe, to hope, to love. These powers you need because without them you cannot live the Christian life to which baptism commits you. But within the common Christian life there are the many-splendored forms of Christian existence. Father or mother, wife or husband, teacher or student, doctor or lawyer, business person or government worker, white collar or blue, robust or infirm—whoever you are, you have a specific vocation right now within the Christian body.

Now that vocation calls indeed for natural skills, gifts of mind or body, of spirit or flesh. But over and above these, it calls for special gifts, graces, empowerments you can expect from God to accomplish your calling as *Christian* servants, to fulfil your vocation for the common good. Not to pile supernatural upon natural (that is a misleading image); rather to make of you one Christian person. Not a person *with* a charism; in the last analysis, the charism is you, the Spirit-inspired you.

Here is a fresh vision of Christian living. The doctor is no longer a Christian engaged in a secular occupation. You are a new incarnation of the healing Christ, can expect to be empowered with gifts that make for a more total healing. A mother is not merely a Christian who raises children for God and society. Each act of mothering, each gesture, is an embodiment of a Christian person, a woman enlivened by God's Spirit. The Christian lawyer is not simply a clever counselor questing for justice. Your admirable love of law must be quickened by an all-embracing law of love. The student or scholar is not only cold intellect seeking knowledge and understanding. You can expect of God a deeper insight into the human mysteries that mystify you, a Christian savor and relish, a delight in the things of God, the people of God, God Himself.

II

So far so good. When the word of God enters your flesh, you are a new incarnation. This integration of human gifts and God's self-giving, this is the remarkable charism that is you. You are unique; there is no other you.

My second point: This "new you" stems from the Holy Spirit. I've already said this, but I want to stress it. You see, there are two unchristian errors at large in our land, two extremes. At one extreme, Pelagianism; at the other, pessimism. The Pelagian is the incurable optimist: He can lift himself to heaven by his bootstraps. No original sin, no need to be reborn; free will can save him, with an occasional nudge from God—your Christian example or a three-point homily. . . . Hogwash! We reach God by God's gracious, uncompelled mercy. Even the clergy do—if they do. And we can work out our specific Christian calling, we can touch Christ to others, only if the Spirit of Christ is living and active within us. To do freely what we ought to do—to believe and hope and love—we need a freedom that flows from the Spirit. Without Him we are literally lost.

The pessimist sins in her own way. She feels she has nothing to offer the community. She is homely or has blackheads; she is shy, insecure, stutters; she can't sing or disco, isn't particularly smart, can't hold her Michelob; blacks scare her and blood makes her throw up. She doesn't like herself. Don't add community to her problems!

A word from your favorite counselor: All is not yet lost. What makes you an effective Christian is the Holy Spirit. Oh yes, personality can be a blessing; it's great if you warm instinctively to people;

it could help if you're a "ten."[3] But more importantly, the Spirit works through you as you are; all He asks is that you be open to His whispering. He illumines your mind to know the way you should go, fortifies your will to go that way despite obstacles without and weakness within. With Him, when you are weak you are strong; for it is He who works in you. He gives you what St. Paul calls "the fruit of the Spirit": He gives you "love, joy, peace, patience, kindness, goodness, faithfulness, gentleness, self-control" (Gal 5:22–23). What more can you want? There are no natural substitutes. You may still need therapy or a skin cream to make you utterly whole; but whoever you are, whatever your infirmities and imperfections, it is the Spirit alone who can make you a means of redemption, a channel of grace, an instrument of God's peace. It is He who changes your water into wine.

III

This leads directly to my third point: The gifts of the Spirit we call charisms are given to you for others. St. Paul's Greek says "for [someone else's] advantage" (1 Cor 12:7), for the common good.[4] Oh yes, a gift of God should do something for *you*, alter your inner self, increase your intimacy with Christ. But that is not the primary purpose of charisms. These are gifts that look beyond you, to your life with others, your existence within a community, your call to minister, to serve.

When I celebrate the Eucharist, the flesh of Christ should indeed feed me; when I preach, I ought to live what I proclaim. But the Eucharist is not my private banquet; the homily is not Hamlet talking to himself. Eucharist and homily look to the community. The same holds true for you. You are not closet Christians; no Christian is an island. Wherever you have been called—to home or campus, courtroom or Congress, office or lab, hospital ward or refugee camp—wherever you are, nearby or at a distance there is another, there are others. The Spirit makes you what you are to help the community become what it ought to be.

Not only the Christian community—the human community. The time has passed when the Christian body can, like Narcissus, fall in love with its own reflection. From this comfortable, friendly, joy-filled liturgy you will walk out into a world that is cold, that smolders with hate, where fear and despair are as common as dust.

Nearby are black ghettos, winos and drug addicts, pushers and prostitutes, young people who hurt and old folk who are awfully lonely. At a distance are starving Cambodian children, screaming Iranian students, Filipino political prisoners, bleeding Afghans. And most of us will go on living as usual. Fifty to eighty million will watch the Steelers shear the Rams in a Pasadena arena; we'll turn the thermostat down to a painless 68; our students will curse the only hamburger with two dimensions—length and width.

I suppose we must if we are not to go mad. I'm not asking you to forgo simple pleasures, to picket the Pub or shower in ice water. I *am* asking you never to wallow in self-pity for what you are not, to recognize that each of you is someone very special, because you have gifts of the Spirit that can speak to others' needs. I *am* asking you to take joy in these gifts. I *am* asking you to touch your gifts to others, to make another life endurable, human, Christian, to surprise others with joy. I *am* suggesting that, unless you and I move out to the other, this dancing Dahlgren community will deserve to die.

Dahlgren Chapel
Georgetown University
January 20, 1980

14
BLESSED ARE YOU?
Sixth Sunday of the Year (C)

- *Jeremiah 17:5–8*
- *1 Corinthians 15:12, 16–20*
- *Luke 6:17, 20–26*

Let's confess it right off: Today we have a tough Gospel. If it didn't shake you, you weren't really listening. Or else you're poor, hungry, sad, and universally hated, and the Gospel promises that your turn is coming. Come the revolution, you'll be rich and fat, you'll be laughing all the time, and everybody will love you. But if your wallet is packed with "bread" and your intestines are flatulent from pizza and beer, if your life is veined with laughter and the world speaks well of you, watch out: You'll get it in the end, literally and figuratively.

To unravel it all should take at least three points, but I propose to try it in two. I want, first, to uncover what St. Luke was saying then, and second, what the Gospel might be saying to you and me now.

I

The first problem is Luke. Why? Because he is so different from Matthew. Luke has four beatitudes, not eight or nine; he does not spiritualize poverty and hunger; and, to make things crystal-clear, he has four woes for the bad guys. On this, a bit of biblical erudition.

First, when Jesus says "Blessed are you," he is not praising you or blessing you. "Blessed are you" means there is something good about your situation. In some sense you are fortunate if you are poor or hungry, saddened or slandered.[1] And when Jesus says "Woe to you," he means there is something not so good about your situation. In some sense you are unfortunate if you are rich or sated, joy-filled or applauded.

Second, Luke does not have, as Matthew does, "Blessed are the poor in spirit" or "Blessed are those who hunger for righteousness" (Mt 5:3, 6). Luke is talking about real poverty, about physical hunger. It does not mean that you must choose between Matthew and Luke, that either Matthew or Luke took liberties with the words of Jesus. More than likely, Luke is closer to what Jesus actually said; Matthew interprets Jesus, stresses what he sees as aspects of poverty and hunger close to the needs of his community.[2]

Third, if Luke's beatitudes burn us, we cats cannot get off the "hot tin roof" the way some scholars do.[3] For them, the poor, the hungry, the sad are men and women with certain spiritual dispositions, an attitude of soul: Unable to help themselves, they look to God for help. Surely some of them do, but this is not what Luke has in mind. His poor are the oppressed, victims of injustice, men and women without human defense. His hungry are the starving, those who have not the nourishment necessary for life, have no way of getting it. His weepers are men and women who have experienced some dread sorrow, serious affliction, so terrible that they must cry aloud what they feel within.

These are the people the prophet Isaiah mentions, the prophecy Jesus saw fulfilled in himself: "The Spirit of the Lord is upon me, because the Lord has anointed me to preach good news to the poor ... to set at liberty the oppressed ... to comfort all who mourn" (Isa 61:1–2; Lk 4:18). The Old Testament and the New spell out who these unfortunates are: the deaf and dumb and blind, lepers and the crippled, exiles and the enslaved, the hungry and homeless, the widow and orphan, the fatigued and heavy-burdened, those broken in heart or crushed in spirit. They are summed up in Luke's parable of Lazarus—the poor, hungry, afflicted Lazarus who dies and is carried off by angels, while the rich man is tormented in Hades (Lk 16:19–31).

Fourth, why did Jesus promise the kingdom of God to these unfortunates? Not because they were holier, better disposed, more devoted to God than the prosperous; some were not. Jesus does not idealize poverty, glorify hunger, canonize tears—no more than he sanctified sin by wearing our sinful flesh. In the beatitudes, as all through the Gospels, Jesus tells us something about *God.*[4]

You see, the ancient East expected its kings to be protectors of the poor and oppressed. Not because these were better citizens than the rest, but because justice-for-all was an essential attribute of kingship. The poor were privileged not because poverty had particular merit, but because a king would not be a genuine king if he did not show special concern for the oppressed, if he did not help the helpless.

In this, the earthly king was modeled on God. For Israel, Yahweh was protector of the poor, defender of the defenseless, not because they were more pious (some were not), not because they trusted in Him alone (some did not), but because God owed it to Himself to assure justice, owed it to His justice to bring about a just kingdom.

But in Israel, as elsewhere, theory was one thing, reality another. Despite Yahweh's solicitude, the poor were hardly better off in Israel than among the pagans. Rather than make an issue of God's justice, the Israelites projected it into the future: God's justice will be revealed one day, when His dazzling intervention will establish His rule over the earth.

In the beatitudes, therefore, we have a theology not of human poverty but of divine justice. The good news is: "The kingdom of God is at hand" (Mk 1:15). Of that kingdom Jesus is God's personal revelation. In him we glimpse the real nature of divine kingship: a "kingship which seeks not to dominate but to save—and to save in the first instance, by pure grace, the men and women who are the most unfortunate, those on whom the consequences of sin weigh most heavily."[5]

The Christian stress was indeed to change. Christians soon would fix their eyes not on God's conduct in establishing His kingdom, but on our conduct if we are to share in that kingdom. In this perspective the poor are privileged not by their oppression but by the qualities of soul that make them profoundly religious and merit for them the recompense to come. This is suggested by the fourth of Luke's beatitudes: Blessed are you when you suffer *for the sake of Christ,* for him on whom your salvation depends. With him as your motive force, with him as your love, you can "rejoice and leap for joy" (Lk 6:23).

II

My second point: What might the Gospel be saying to you and me now? How would we rephrase Luke's beatitudes today? Try your hand at it. It could be a profound experience; it might even disclose what sort of Christian you are. Let me try my beatitudes on you. Call it my Sermon not on the Mount but on the Hilltop.

What do I say to the 60 million poor in America, to the Indian subcontinent where 200 million live on less than 40 dollars a year? What do I say to the 460 million who at this moment are starving, to Cambodian babies whose minds and bodies are already beyond repair, to the billion who go to bed hungry each night? What do I say to those who never laugh, who cannot laugh—political prisoners in the Philippines or the Gulag Archipelago, maimed women and children in Northern Ireland, Palestinian expatriates, the raped in Afghanistan and the hostages in Iran, the blacks in D.C. slums?

Dare I say "Blessed are you," you are in a fortunate situation? In some ways, yes. Blessed are you because God loves you, because Christ has a special place in his heart for the oppressed, the disinherited. Blessed are you because somehow—I know not how—somehow the blessings of God's kingdom will be yours; sometime—I know not when—sometime you will laugh and leap for joy. Blessed are you because now God alone can fill your emptiness. Blessed are you because you prick my conscience, because you reveal to me my nakedness, my poverty in God's eyes, my borderline Christianity, my refusal to give you my "cloak as well," to go the extra mile, to "give to him who begs" (Mt 6:40–42). Blessed are you because you are living the crucified Christ I constantly avoid.

From this hilltop it is easier to say "Woe." Luke might say it baldly: Woe to you who are rich in money, because you profit from a sinful social structure. Woe to you who are rich in intelligence, because you waste it like the prodigal or use it only to get richer. Woe to you who are rich in time, because you squander it in self-pity or to get "bombed." Woe to you who are well-fed, because you are "a privileged part of the way food is unequally spread among humans."[6] Woe to you who are filled, because you rarely experience your real emptiness. Woe to you who laugh, because you joy not in the gifts of the Spirit, you joy in what you have made of yourself.

But I would rather turn the woes around. Blessed are you rich, rich in money or power, in talent or time, because you can do so much for the poor, can lift the yoke of the oppressed. But blessed only if you have the mind of the poor, the mind of Christ. Only if you recognize that you may not do what you will with what you have. Only if you realize that you are stewards, that whatever you have you hold in trust—from God for man. Only if you are not enslaved to your riches, do not place your trust in them. Only if you experience in some way the poverty of the poor, the oppression of the oppressed. Only if you are ready to lose all you have for the sake of Christ, for your brothers and sisters. Blessed are you rich, if you are ready to follow the naked Christ naked.

Blessed are you who are full now, who are sleek and well-fed, because you are strong enough to feed the hungry, to touch empty stomachs with compassion. But blessed only if you have the mind of the hungry, the mind of Christ. Only if you do not take your food for granted. Only if you are uncomfortable as long as one brother or sister cries in vain for bread or justice or love. Only if you experience what hunger tastes like. Only if you experience your own profound emptiness—how desperately you need the hungry, how far you still are from God. Blessed are the full, if you are always hungry.

Blessed are you who laugh now, because you can bring the joy of Christ to others, to those whose days are woven of tears. But blessed only if you can laugh at yourselves, if you don't take yourselves too seriously, if human living doesn't revolve around you and your needs. Only if you take delight in all God's creation—in sun and surf, in snow and star, in blue marlin and robin redbreast, in Cézanne and Ronstadt and Veal Scallopine, in the love of man or maid and the presence of Trinity within you. Only if laughter means that you let go—let go of all that shackles you to yesterday, imprisons you in your small selves. Blessed are you who laugh, because you are free.

A final word—to rich and poor, to full and empty, to laugher and weeper. A final word: Be not afraid. Unreal? Perhaps. But only if, as Jeremiah has it, you put your trust not in the Lord but in flesh. Then indeed you will live "a barren bush on the desert," inherit woe "in a salt and empty earth" (Jer 17:6). But if God is your "refuge and strength," then you "will not fear though the earth should change, . . . though the mountains tremble" (Ps 46:1–3).

Only then will you risk all, literally all, not for today's joy but for tomorrow's kingdom. Not optimism but hope.

It is time for you, each of you, to ask yourself a question: What are my beatitudes?

Dahlgren Chapel
Georgetown University
February 17, 1980

15
WHO TOUCHED ME?
Thirteenth Sunday of the Year (B)

- *Wisdom 1:13–15; 2:23–24*
- *2 Corinthians 8:7, 9, 13–15*
- *Mark 5:21–43*

In the middle of today's Gospel there is an uncommonly moving scene (Mk 5:25–34). A woman whose life has been bleeding away for twelve years pushes through a tremendous crowd, comes up behind Jesus, touches his garment. Instantly the bleeding ceases; she feels in her body that she has been healed. Jesus is aware that power has gone forth from him; he quickly asks: "Who touched my garments?" The disciples are amazed, almost amused: "You see the crowd pressing around you, and yet you say 'Who touched me?' " But he keeps looking around, keeps looking until the woman comes in fear and trembling and tells him the whole truth. And Jesus explains to her what has happened: "Daughter, your faith has made you well; go in peace. . . ."

"Who touched me?" Three years ago, for the first time, that question laid hold of me, made me shiver. I cannot get it out of my mind. Increasingly it has told me something: something about Jesus, something about myself, something about Christian living. A word about each.

I

First, the question "Who touched me?" tells me something about Jesus. Physical touch dots the life of Jesus. Not only the

woman with the hemorrhage, but so many of the sick he cured and
the dead he raised—so often he touched them. The dead twelve-
year-old girl in today's Gospel (Mk 5:41); Peter's fevered mother-
in-law (Mt 8:15); a leper (Mt 8:3); blind men (Mt 10:29–30); a deaf
man with a speech defect (Mk 7:33); an epileptic boy (Mk 9:27); the
"sick with various diseases" (Lk 5:40); a woman bent over for eigh-
teen years (Lk 13:13); the high priest's slave whose ear Peter cut off
(Jn 18:10; Lk 22:51)—all of these he touched. When Peter was
sinking in the sea, Jesus "reached out his hand and caught him"
(Mt 14:31). Children he not only blessed; he "took them in his
arms" (Mk 10:16). At the Last Supper he lovingly washed the feet
of his disciples (Jn 13:5).

And Jesus let others touch him: the sick at Gennesaret (Mt
14:36); the crowds (Lk 6:19); the sinful woman who "wet his feet
with her tears" and dried them with her hair (Lk 8:38); Mary Magdalene after the Resurrection (Jn 20:17). He even invited Thomas
to touch his wounds (Jn 20:27).

I am not saying that Jesus was a hail-fellow-well-met, a back-
slapper, a "gimme some skin" type. I *am* saying that this man,
whose life was compassion and love, was not satisfied with words,
even compassionate and loving words. The same man who gave his
body to a bloody death on a cross did not hold that flesh aloof, in
splendid isolation from "the madding crowd's ignoble strife." It
was not a disembodied spirit that attracted Peter and Magdalene,
cured the sick and resurrected the dead, ate with sinners and drove
sellers from the Temple, responded to the needs of so many different people. His tears and his touch were as much part of his saving
presence, his redemptive action, as his words and his prayers. How
expressive his touch must have been—the touch of God on our
skin! How consoling, how comforting, how strengthening!

II

Second, the question "Who touched me?" tells me something
about myself. Decades ago, as I grew up in the Christian community and in religious life, touch was a dangerous creature. The stress,
in philosophy and theology, in asceticism and spirituality, was on
the powers that set us above the beast: mind and will, intelligence
and freedom. The life of the senses was genuine life, of course; but
seeing and hearing, smelling and tasting and touching were ave-

nues to *understanding,* the way we mortals had to go to reach *ideas,* ideas that would spark rational decisions. The emotions, the passions were undeniably part and parcel of human experience; but they were perilous. They had been unleashed by Adam's sin, were no longer under our despotic control.

In this context touch had a special place. It was the tinder that could kindle passion. Rough-and-tumble touch—the hockey check, the football tackle, the sweaty arm around the shoulder, even the swift pat on the rump—no problem. Touch within marriage—no barriers whatsoever, as long as conception was not impeded. But outside such situations, touch was a dangerous devil; it was hard to segregate it from sinful sex.

I do not want to caricature the past. Nor do I want to deny the latent power of touch; quite the contrary. What I do regret is that our emphasis on the threat in touch played down the extraordinary essence of touch. It was years before I realized that touch is communication; touch *says* something—and says it in a way no other human power can rival.

With a touch I tell you I care . . . I like you . . . I love you . . . I'm sorry for your troubles . . . I rejoice in your joy . . . I share your sadness, your weakness, your pain . . . I understand . . . I don't know what to say . . . I congratulate you . . . I bless you . . . I accept you . . . I know how you feel . . . I'm lonely . . . I need you . . . I want you sexually. And so on and so forth. There is little that touch cannot say.

And touch finds it difficult to lie. I can weave *words* in such fashion that I deceive you, that my mind and my heart do not really lie open to you. But I can rarely if ever program touch that way; it will not obey me, it simply translates me.

Which leads to a broader issue still. Physical touch tells others in a uniquely powerful way what I am, who I am. This fact suggests to me what my whole life should be: touching and being touched. Not only the touch of my hand or my lips, but a whole web of relationships. It tells me that life is communication; to be alive is to communicate; the very word means to share; life is a giving and receiving. Life is exchange. In Rosemary Haughton's beautiful words:

> [Creation itself is an exchange.] Sit on a hillside and look at the wild flowers and the trees below you. Each draws life from the

soil, from the sun, from the rain. It grows, leafs, flowers, fruits.
Its leaves fall, it dies and becomes part of the soil. The plants
can grow only from the soil, the living soil can be made only
from the plants. This is exchange of life.

. . . Speech and meaning exist only in exchange. I receive
meaning and I give it back, with something of "myself" in it.
This is exchange of life.

What is "myself," then? I live only in exchange [chemical
and biological, thought and feeling]. [And] because I am human,
[I] recognize myself as being in exchange. I receive life and give
it back, at all levels—physical, cultural and spiritual interchang-
ing with one another.

[Further,] my "being in exchange" is the image of the ultimate and perfect Exchange, the life of God.

The theology of the Trinity is the assertion that the very being of God is exchange—a total and absolute outpouring of being, a total and absolute acceptance of being, a total and
absolute giving back of that received being; and the very name
of that exchange is Love, the Very Being of God. There is no
claiming, no possessing, but eternal and utter giving and receiving.[1]

Who touched me? Whom have I touched? Why, God; countless men, women, and children; even the "things" that God and
others have made. My whole life is touch, because my whole life is
exchange. The tragedy lies in not recognizing this, not living it
consciously, not making my life increasingly an exchange.

III

Third, the question "Who touched me?" tells me something
about Christian living. Actually, I have already indicated this; for I
have suggested that *human* living is an exchange, a touching and
being touched. Let me merely make this more obviously Christian
on three levels: the touch of Christ, the sacramental touch, and the
touch of Christian love.

Christian living, at its root, I find admirably symbolized in the
Gospel story of the bleeding woman. Jesus Christ is here, is really
present among us. That living presence makes it possible for me to
reach out to him, to touch the hem of his garment. If I do, he turns
to me, looks for me, wants me to know him, yearns to live in me.
The faith I showed in touching him begins to make me whole. It is
the overture of an exchange that should mark my whole life.

But notice, I could never reach out to him, did he not already reach out to me. It is St. Augustine's remarkable insight: If we but turn to God, that is itself a gift of God. Very simply, grace is God giving Himself to me in Ch st, I in response giving myself to God through Christ. The life of grace is a life of exchange. God and I touch.

This touch of Christ finds a physical reflection in our sacramental system. Here is a ceaseless touching that gives life, that heals, that makes two one. I touch water to a freshly born girl, and God's life streams through her. A bishop lays hands on a young man, oils him with chrism, and a new outpouring of the Spirit empowers him to witness to his faith even unto crucifixion. I touch a fellow sinner with words of forgiveness, and he takes up his infirmities and walks again. I anoint a sick body, and God's life strengthens frail flesh and suffering spirit. A bishop's hands grip a young man's head, and he rises priested, to celebrate life and mediate it to a people. I touch to a hand what looks like bread, touch to lips what looks like wine, and fragile flesh ingests eternal life. A man and a woman link hands to symbolize their endless oneness, and in so touching they touch God to each other.

Now the touch of Christ and the sacramental touch should be reflected in our human exchange, in the touch of this Christian body. We must, Christ told us, love one another as he has loved us (cf. Jn 15:12). This demands that I take the initiative in loving; I dare not wait to be loved. Remember the First Epistle of John: "In this is love, not that we loved God but that He loved us and sent His Son to be the expiation for our sins" (1 Jn 4:10). It is my Christian responsibility, my Christian calling, to reach out and touch another pulsing person. At times it will mean physical touch—more often perhaps than we think. But even here the touch of my hand or my arm, my lips or my body, should be expressive of something deeper, fuller, richer: It is a symbol of my whole self. *I* touch you—not simply my hand. And because I am touching you with my love, I am touching to you the love of Christ.

But though I take the initiative in touching, in loving, Christian touch, like all human touch, is not one-sided; it is an exchange. In touching, I am touched. Remember St. Francis of Assisi: "It is in giving that we receive." Whether it is my hand or my heart that reaches out to another, I not only *give* life, I *get* life. Somewhat as I cannot have God's life unless I live off the vine that is Christ, neither can I live as a Christian unless I receive life and love from the body that is Christ—from you.

For me, one of the fresh marvels of Holy Communion is that I not only distribute Communion to you; your eyes meet mine; there is not only your communion with Christ, but at the same time your communion with me. You receive from me and I receive from you.

More importantly, when you leave this altar, will the presence of the same sacramental Christ within you make you more aware of the faithful around you, the men, women, and children with whom you exchange life on so many levels, without whom you would be less alive, less human, less Christian? And when you leave this chapel, will the touch of Christ and this worshiping community open you to those who need your touch because they need your life, your love? Not the "boat people" in far-off Malaysia; someone on your street, in your house, on your corridor. It is a thrilling experience to see budding on another's face that wondering, wondrous question "Who touched me?" and to realize it was not so much you as Christ within you. More thrilling still, when you reach out that way, it is often you who are surprised by joy, you who ask in wonderment "Who touched *me?*"

Dahlgren Chapel
Georgetown University
July 1, 1979

16
WHEN HE SAW HIM, HE HAD COMPASSION
Fifteenth Sunday of the Year (C)

- *Deuteronomy 30:10–14*
- *Colossians 1:15–20*
- *Luke 10:25–37*

The story of the Good Samaritan has vexed me for over a month. Why? Because I had difficulty deciding what to draw from it for your Christian existence—and mine. Let me tell you, first, what I planned originally to do and decided not to; second, what suddenly struck me as a more important point to make; third, what this might tell us about God, about Jesus, and about ourselves.

I

Originally I had different plans for this homily. I was going to answer the question put to Jesus by the lawyer: "And who is my neighbor?" (Lk 10:29). I would tell you, clearly and eloquently, who your neighbor is.

It all seemed so simple. Your neighbor? Why, your neighbors are the patients I recently read about in the *Washington Post:* a hundred and eleven elderly or disabled men and women in D.C. General. They don't need a hospital, but they have no place to go: no home to return to, no nursing home open. Over fifty have not had a visitor for a year; sixty percent will leave the hospital only when they die.

Who is your neighbor? Why, the countless refugees from

Cambodia—thousands of women and children ravaged by dysentery, tuberculosis, malaria. The Brazilian farmers for whom John Paul wept: men who make ten dollars a month, families that live in shacks fashioned of planks and cardboard. The doctors and nurses machine-gunned by police in El Salvador. The elderly husband and wife whose welfare check will no longer buy inflated hamburger or depressed chicken. The blind and the halt, the cancer-ridden and the imprisoned. The lonely people on your street, on your campus.

This *was* to be the heart of my homily, but it will not be. These are indeed your neighbors, because if you are human, nothing that is human is a stranger to you; and if you are Christian, everything human is part and parcel of you. On the other hand, I cannot really tell you who the neighbor is to whom *you* must show compassion. Only you know that—you with your eyes opened by God's grace, you in your particular situation, in your concrete existence. Not mine to define your individual Christian duty; not mine to lay a guilt trip on you.

II

Let me rather take my cue from Jesus' own question. The lawyer had asked: "Who is my neighbor?" Whom must I treat as a friend? What are the limits of my responsibility?[1] Whom can I exclude? Foreigners? Non-Pharisees? The sons of darkness? Heretics? Personal enemies? Jesus asks: "Which of these three proved to be a neighbor?" (Lk 10:36). The question has moved from the object of mercy to its subject. The focus is no longer on the one who hurts but on the one who heals. The problem is . . . I. And that problem revolves around a single verb: The Samaritan, when he saw the Jew beaten half to death, "had compassion" (v. 33).

In biblical Greek this is a remarkable word. It is remarkable, first, for what it means. You know how you and I speak of the heart as the seat and source of our emotions, our feelings. If I am frightened, my heart is in my mouth. If I am depressed, my heart is in my boots. If I love you, I love you with all my heart. If I weep for you, my heart goes out to you. For the same purpose, the Jews used a figure that sounds strange to us. Where we say "heart," they often said "bowels." They spoke especially of the bowels of love and affection, the bowels of mercy and sympathy and compassion. For as with us, so with them, these are feelings that come from deep within us. They are not cold thoughts; they are born in the depths of our being, and when they are torn from us, expelled, expressed, we joy or agonize.

There is something still more remarkable about this biblical word for compassion. When it is used in the Gospels, it is used only of God the Father or of Jesus the Christ. In his famous song of praise, the father of John the Baptist extols the "bowels of mercy of our God" (Lk 1:78); the king [of heaven] forgives the servant in debt to him "out of the bowels of his compassion" (Mt 18:27); the father of the prodigal—really God the Father—runs to meet his repentant son because he is "moved by the bowels of his compassion" (Lk 15:20).

Similarly for Jesus. This strong word strikes us when Jesus has compassion on crowds that are hungry (Mt 15:32), crowds that include the sick (Mt 14:14), crowds that are "harassed and helpless, like sheep without a shepherd" (Mt 9:36); compassion on a leper (Mk 1:41) and on two blind men (Mt 20:34); compassion on a father and his epileptic boy (Mk 9:22), on a mother who has lost her only son (Lk 7:13).

Yes, this strong expression, "bowels of compassion," the Gospels use of God the Father and His only Son. There is but one exception: the Good Samaritan. When the Samaritan came upon the wounded Jew, "he was moved by the bowels of compassion" (Lk 10:33). Like God, like the God-man, the Samaritan "sympathized" to the depths of his being. I suggest that this tells us something significant about God, about Jesus, and about ourselves.

III

It tells us something about God. It may well be true that in the Father, as the Epistle of James declares, "there is no variation or shadow due to change" (Jas 1:17). But it is just as true that this changeless God loves us, has compassion for our woundedness, in the only way God can: I mean, with the whole of His being, the totality of His Godness. On this, Scripture is eloquent. Psalm 103 is but one example:

The Lord is merciful and gracious,
  slow to anger and abounding in steadfast love. . . .
He does not deal with us according to our sins,

> nor requite us according to our iniquities.
> For as the heavens are high above the earth,
>   so great is His steadfast love. . . .
> As a father has compassion on his children,
>   so the Lord has compassion on those who fear Him.
>   (Ps 103:8–13)

This is the loving Lord who proclaimed to a despairing Israel: "As I live, I have no pleasure in the death of the wicked, but that the wicked turn back from his way and live" (Ezek 33:11). This is the God who protests to us when we feel forsaken: "Can a woman forget her sucking child, that she should have no compassion on the son of her womb? Even these may forget, yet I will not forget you" (Isa 49:15).

In Jesus God's compassion took flesh. You see, Jesus is not merely a wonderfully compassionate man, a soft touch for every brand of human misery. He is, in the pregnant and profound expression of Scripture, "God with us." God . . . with . . . us. In him God enters history as a suffering God, a God who wore our weakness, felt our fright, swallowed our bitter cup of rejection and loneliness. On this the Epistle to the Hebrews is eloquent: "We have not a high priest who cannot sympathize with our weaknesses, but one who in every respect has been tempted as we are. . . . He can deal gently with those who sin in ignorance and go astray, because he himself is beset with weakness. . . . In the days of his flesh, Jesus offered up prayers and supplications, with loud cries and tears, to Him who was able to save him from death, and he was heard for his godly fear. Although he was Son, he learned obedience through what he suffered" (Heb 4:15—5:8). The compassion of Jesus is not a virtue he plucked now and again from a pigeonhole and applied to needy cases. He is compassion incarnate, God's compassion in weak human flesh. Everything he did, living or dying, welled up from the bowels of his compassion.

Doesn't this say something to you? If to be a Christian is to put on Christ, then to be a Christian is to clothe yourself in his compassion. You can discuss till doomsday exactly where you should play the Good Samaritan: in Thailand or D.C. General, on campus or at home. After all, much of the world has "fallen among robbers" (Lk 10:30) and most of the wounded you must "pass by on the other side" (v. 31). What is beyond argument is what your heart should feel like . . . or your bowels!

It's not so much a question of your own inner hurt. As time goes on, you experience increasingly what Christ went through— possibly more. For all its rock and roll, for all its quiet joys and occasional ecstasies, human living can tear you apart. The question is, how does this affect you? What does it do to you? Does the bittersweet of human existence lock you into yourself, make you captive to your own misery, so that nothing matters save your loss or your loneliness, your inner insecurity or your spastic colon? Or does your hurt, like the tears of Jesus, open you up to others, unlock the bowels of your compassion? Because you are "beset with weakness," do you "deal gently" with the weak? If you cannot go to Southeast Asia, can you feel the anguish of the Cambodian mother cradling the rigid body of her dead child? If you cannot visit D.C. General, can you experience the emptiness of those old folk who have no future, no present, only memories? If slums are not your "way to go," do you ever sense inside you what it must feel like to be hungry, ignorant, unloved, with only hate and envy in your heart?

To feel hurt is to be human; to link that hurt to others is to be Christlike. But the compassion of the God-man is not only your model to imitate; it is the very source and possibility of your compassion. Your compassion not only *reflects* his; it is a sharing therein, a sharing in the compassion of God. He makes it possible. The Gospel "Go and do likewise" (Lk 10:37) is not addressed to your native, natural, inborn powers. The command is at the same time a gift. And the gift is the compassionate God deep within you, the God who alone can change you, alone can fashion bowels of compassion. Look to Him during this liturgy, especially as you murmur, to Him and to the world's wounded: "This is my body, which is given for you."

Dahlgren Chapel
Georgetown University
July 13, 1980

17
HOW LITTLE WORTHY. . . .
Twenty-fourth Sunday of the Year (A)

- *Sirach 27:30—28:7*
- *Romans 14:7–9*
- *Matthew 18:21–35*

Today's Gospel parable is a gripping story. Like so many of Jesus' parables, there is more to it than meets the naked eye. So let me, first, sketch what the story seems to be saying; second, suggest something significant that lies beneath the surface; third, open the parable to your own Christian imagining.

I

First, what does the parable of the debtors seem to be saying? On the sheer face of it, what is the story about? How does it sound if you just listen to it? What lesson does it plainly leave with you? Very simply, the parable preaches forgiveness. It tells you how to deal with those who owe you something.

The story has three main characters: a king and two servants. One servant owes the king a colossal sum: in our money, about ten million dollars. He cannot possibly repay this, for all his tearful promise: "Give me time and I'll pay back everything." Impossible, and the king knows it. "Out of pity" he cancels the debt, every last dollar.

So what does our grateful debtor do as he skips out of "Caesar's palace" ahead by ten million? He runs into another servant, a chap who owes *him* money. How much? About twenty dollars. Does he tell him to forget it—it's a great day for debtors? No, he grabs him by the throat, chokes him: "Pay me what you owe me!" The poor fellow pleads on his knees: "Give me time and I'll pay you back." Oh no, into prison with you till you raise the twenty!

The king hears the sad story from other servants. He summons servant number one, tells him in anger: "I canceled your ten-million-dollar debt out of compassion for you. Shouldn't you have done the same for twenty dollars?" And the king jails him till he can pay the ten million. Presumably, for life.

The lesson? It's spelled out clearly. You had better forgive your brothers and sisters; otherwise God will not forgive you, will put you away till you pay the last penny you owe Him. The lesson is summed up in today's Old Testament reading from Sirach: "Forgive your neighbor the wrong he [or she] has done, and then your sins will be pardoned when you pray" (Sir 28:2).

II

Second, what lies beneath the surface of this story? I am not retracting the obvious lesson: We should forgive one another. I am suggesting that the obvious lesson may blind us to something more important still, a facet of the story that gives meaning to forgiveness, makes it a Christian virtue. There is indeed a threat: Unless you forgive, God will not forgive you. But there is more, something wonderfully positive. It tells us more profoundly why we should forgive. It tells us something about God.

The parable tells us what the Old Testament repeats tirelessly—what Alexander Pope said so simply: "to forgive [is] divine."[1] The Lord proclaims to Moses on Sinai: "The Lord, the Lord, a God merciful and gracious . . . forgiving iniquity and transgression and sin . . ." (Exod 34:6-7). The Psalms proclaim "a forgiving God" (Ps 99:8), a God "who forgives all your iniquity" (Ps 103:3). The prophet Micah asks: "Who is a God like thee, pardoning iniquity and passing over transgression for the remnant of His inheritance?" (Mic 7:18).

Oh yes, conditions had to be met. To be forgiven, the Israelites had to confess their sin to God; they had to be converted, return to Him; and they had to ask forgiveness. They had to pray with the Psalmist:

Have mercy on me, O God,
    according to thy steadfast love;
according to thy abundant mercy

blot out my transgressions.
Wash me thoroughly from my iniquity,
    and cleanse me from my sin. . . .
Against thee, thee only, have I sinned,
    and done that which is evil in thy sight. . . .
Create in me a clean heart, O God,
    and put a new and right spirit within me.
                            (Ps 51:1–10)

But why should God forgive at all? Moses pleads with Him on the ground of His covenant love: "Pardon the iniquity of this people, I pray thee, according to the greatness of thy steadfast love." And the Lord responds: "I have pardoned, according to your word" (Num 14:19–20). God forgave because He is a God of love who was faithful to His people however often the people broke faith with Him.

And so it is in the New Testament. Recall St. Paul: "As the Lord has forgiven you, so you also must forgive" (Col 3:13). The one difference is that here forgiveness comes through the God-man. It comes especially through his redeeming death: "Drink of it, all of you; for this is my blood of the [new] covenant, which is poured out . . . for the forgiveness of sins" (Mt 26:28). And the forgiveness is free gift, not wrung from God by merit or repentance. It is the gift of a crucified God, faithful to his covenant despite all our infidelities.

Precisely here is the motive for our own forgiving. We are to be merciful, not because a brother or sister merits our mercy, but because the Lord has been merciful to us—unto death. We are to forgive, not because the debtor deserves forgiveness, but because the God-man has forgiven us. "Be merciful," Jesus said in the Sermon on the Plain, "even as your Father is merciful" (Lk 6:36). Be compassionate as He is compassionate, He who gave His Son for sin. We too have a covenant, not only with God but with one another in Christ. In that covenant we forgive because we have been forgiven.

In short, the more important lesson of the parable, the lesson that stems from Israel's history and touches our own, is surely the question put by the king to the unforgiving servant: "Should not you have had mercy on your fellow servant, as I had mercy on you?" (Mt 18:33). As I had mercy on you. As God had mercy on us.

III

Third, let me open the parable to your own Christian imagining. I say "your own" because it is not my task to tell you precisely what to do, how to lead your individual lives, whom to forgive and how. It is not mine to say to a survivor of Auschwitz: Forgive the Nazi who gassed your parents. Not mine to counsel a rape victim: Forgive and forget. Not mine to insist that you sit down and cancel every debt owed you. A homily, like a parable, has different lessons for different listeners, different strokes for different folks. In fact, the conclusion of today's parable, "So also my heavenly Father will do to every one of you, if you do not forgive your brother from your heart" (v. 35), is probably Matthew's own application, may well reflect his "legalistic tendency."[2] My function is to help you to see Jesus—not with my eyes but with yours; to open your ears to his voice, to what *he* is saying to you. And this, believe it or not, Jesus does not clear in advance with the homilist!

Still, there is something I do want to say, simply to stimulate your own imagining, your personal response to Jesus. Each of you should be merciful primarily because each of you has received mercy. Unless, like Mary, you were immaculately conceived—and the odds against that are "off the board"—God washed you in baptism from "the sin of the world," graced you in Christ. You owe God. Even if you've never swerved an inch from the straight and narrow—possible, but I wouldn't bet on it—the reason you haven't is not your natural goodness, your "divine" personality, your ability to lift yourself to heaven by your bootstraps; it is God's gift. You owe God. You are remarkably Christian; this I know from experience, and not only because you like three-point homilies. But you are as you are only because, as St. Augustine insisted, if we but turn to God, that itself is a gift of God. You owe God.

Owing God calls not for guilt but for gratitude. The gratitude will be genuine if you are compassionate as your heavenly Father is compassionate. How? Again, different strokes for different folks. For Mother Teresa, it's the skeletons in Calcutta. For some Georgetown students, it's the refugees in Thailand. For Franciscan Father Bruce Ritter, it's the sewers of Times Square. In a single year 12,000 kids ask his help—scared kids, burned, pimped and prostituted, overdosed and angel-dusted.

But for most of us compassion is not so dramatic. We deal not with the down-and-out but with the "up-and-in." Yet they too call for our caring. The trouble is, we tend to dole out our love (including our forgiving) to those who can prove they deserve it, those we like, those who say "thanks," those who may repay kindness in kind, those we can count on to return the six-pack. Jesus blasted that sort of love: Even the detested tax collectors did that, even the idolatrous Gentiles (Mt 5:46–47).

No, in forgiving, in caring, in loving, we are not to look at human merit, a man or woman's worth. Oh yes, the human in anyone should strike a spark in us. But more importantly, we look at God and we remember that, without any merit of our own, we have experienced His forgiveness: He has canceled a debt infinitely greater than the servant's ten million dollars. "Should you not have compassion on your brothers and sisters, as I [God] had compassion on you?"

Sometimes it takes a personal crisis to make us see that "merit" is not the Christian motive for forgiveness, for caring. At times we have to be bruised and battered, brought to our knees, forced to face up to our own undeserving. Jesus reconciled us to God through his cross. Perhaps we may come to Christian caring through our own cross, when we confront our own vulnerability, when we cry out in pain for a cup of cold water, for a gentle hand, for a voice that cares, when we discover with the poet Francis Thompson "how little worthy of any love" we are.[3] How little worthy. . . .

Dahlgren Chapel
Georgetown University
September 13, 1981

18
I'M THE GREATEST!
Twenty-fifth Sunday of the Year (B)

- *Wisdom 2:12, 17–20*
- *James 3:16—4:3*
- *Mark 9:30–37*

A funny thing happened on the way to Capernaum. A group of grown men—at least twelve—had a serious argument. What were they arguing about? Not who had caught the biggest fish; not who had the bushiest beard or the mightiest muscles, the bluest eyes or the bluest blood. No, they were debating which of them was the most important!

Now these were not Middle East oil exporters or White House staffers. They were men who had been chosen by God-in-flesh to be his intimate circle, to spread his good news, to proclaim to Israel that its redemption was at hand. In telling the story, Mark gives no details; but I can almost hear Andrew telling his brother Peter: "I saw him before you did." And Peter retorting: "Okay, but he gave *me* the keys." And James interjecting: "Don't forget, he took *me* up the mountain to meet Moses and Elias. Only three of us saw that; the rest of you guys ain't seen nuthin'." And Judas with the last word: "Argue all you want, he gave *me* the money box. And if you've got the money, you've got it all—no moola, no Manischewitz!"

Fantastic! It's "the odd couple" multiplied, a host of Muhammed Ali's in a new show called "I'm the Greatest." But at least they had the good sense to be embarrassed when the Master asked: "What were you discussing on the way?" They had the good sense to say nothing. But it didn't really help. They were given a brief but pungent lesson: "Do you want to know what it means to be first? It means to be last; it means to be the servant of everyone else" (cf. Mk 9:35).

But what does this mean—for today's disciple as well as yesterday's apostle? What does it mean to be "servant of all"? First a word about Jesus, then a word about ourselves.

I

A word about Jesus. Here two New Testament themes strike me as especially pertinent. First, the word Mark uses in our Gospel passage to express "servant" is the word from which our English "deacon" descends. It has a fascinating history in the New Testament. It is used of the waiters who serve the water-made-wine at Cana's marriage feast (Jn 2:5, 9). Matthew uses it of the king's servants in the parable of the marriage feast (Mt 22:13). It is St. Paul's way of describing himself: He is servant of the gospel (Col 1:23; Eph 3:7), servant of the Church (Col 1:25), servant of the new covenant in the Spirit (2 Cor 3:6), servant of God through much affliction (2 Cor 6:4). John uses it of Jesus' adherents in general; they are his "deacons," his servants: "where I am, there shall my servant be also" (Jn 12:26). The First Letter of Peter claims that all Christians should employ, literally "deacon," the many-splendored charisms they have from God for the advantage of one another, "as good stewards of God's dappled grace" (1 Pet 4:10). And Jesus tells us—using the same language—that he himself did not come on earth to be served; he came to serve (Mt 20:28; Mk 10:45).

Beautiful indeed, touching; but it still does not tell us what it *means* to serve—to serve the gospel, the Church, the covenant, God, one another. Here, I suggest, a second New Testament theme is splendidly revealing. Very early in the life of the Church,[1] Jesus was seen as the Suffering Servant of Yahweh of whom Isaiah sang:

> He was despised and rejected by men,
>   a man of sorrows, and acquainted with grief. . . .
> Surely he has borne our griefs and carried our sorrows. . . .
> He was wounded for our transgressions,
>   he was bruised for our iniquities;
> upon him was the chastisement that made us whole,
>   and with his stripes we are healed.

All we like sheep have gone astray;
   we have turned, everyone, to his own way;
and the Lord has laid on him
   the iniquity of us all.
He was oppressed, and he was afflicted.
   yet he opened not his mouth,
like a lamb that is led to the slaughter. . . .
When he makes himself an offering for sin,
he shall see his offspring . . .
shall see the fruit of the travail of his soul
   and be satisfied. . . .

                    (Isa 53:3–11)

On this Servant Song the early Church meditated; in this servant the early Church discovered Jesus. And it was in the context of this meditation and this discovery that St. Paul understood, if he did not compose,[2] the lyrical Christological hymn we find in his letter to the Christians of Philippi:

Though of divine status,
he did not treat like a miser's booty
his right to be like God
[his right to appear like Yahweh in glory],
but emptied himself of it,
to take up the status of a slave
and become like men;
having assumed human form,
he still further humbled himself
with an obedience that meant death—
even death upon a cross!

                    (Phil 2:6–8)[3]

What did service mean for this servant? Obedience . . . humiliation . . . death. Obedience: "I have come down from heaven not to do my own will, but the will of Him who sent me" (Jn 6:38). Humiliation: "I tell you that this scripture must be fulfilled in me, 'And he was reckoned with transgressors' " (Lk 22:37; see Isa 53:12).[4] Death: "This is my blood of the covenant, which is poured out for many for the forgiveness of sins" (Mt 26:28). In fact, Jesus expressly linked his serving to his dying: "The Son of Man came not to be served but to serve, and to give his life as a ransom for many" (Mt 20:28; Mk 10:45).

II

Now how does the servant Jesus touch our service? Intimately. For "a disciple is not above his [or her] teacher, nor a servant above his [or her] master" (Mt 10:24). To be a disciple of Jesus is not simply to spread his message; it means living his life. To be a servant of Jesus is not merely to light the candles or pass the cookies, not only to be kind to the wrinkled or hold hands with the despairing. And surely the Christian servant is not the British butler of TV, who serves indeed but in his heart knows he is better than his betters and in the privacy of his pantry looks down his proud nose at them.

Christian service is Christ's service. And so it involves, in the first place, obedience. I am not talking about individual acts of submission—to pope or president, to parent or pastor, to employer or provost, even to the omnipotent director of campus ministry. At bottom, to be obedient is to be open. Open to what *God* might ask of you, might be asking of you now—a God who calls in unexpected ways, to unexpected service. A God who called septuagenarian Abraham to father His nation and teen-age Mary to mother His Son; called low-income fishermen and a tax collector to preach freedom to the world; asked twelve-year-old Agnes and eighty-six-year-old Polycarp to shed their blood for Him; asked Antony to quit the city and Augustine to humanize it; called Mother Teresa to cradle the dregs of Calcutta and Father Damien to join literally the lepers of Molokai; calls millions of nameless Christians to lose life in order to save it, to give their lives as a ransom, a redemption, for many. This unpredictable God even asks some strange characters to become Jesuits!

You see, you will hardly be a servant of Christ if your options are closed, if your tomorrows are so programed that there is no room for the unexpected. No, to be Christ's servant is to be as open as he was: "Not my will but thine." Whatever it is, wherever it leads. Only in this way will you be open to the men and women who need the gifts God has given you, need your hands or your heart, your wisdom or your strength, your love and your compassion.

Second, humiliation. I don't mean simply to turn the other cheek: "Hit me again." The primary way Christ humbled himself was in emptying himself. He put off the trappings of divinity, "his right to be like God," put himself in our condition, became like us. Don't wait for others to humble you. Christian life is a constant kenosis, a self-emptying, a putting off of yesterday. Why? To join the human race of today. My yesterdays have indeed shaped me, from honorary degrees to an untamed colon. But I dare not live in yesterday. Especially must I put off what made me so special yesterday, all those things that spelled difference and division, that severed me, distanced me, from my brothers and sisters. Like Jesus, I must be increasingly aware of my solidarity with every man and every woman. I mean that awareness of sameness which made Thomas Merton feel so free, made him laugh with joy, made him cry in his heart: "Thank God, thank God that I *am* like other men, that I am only a man among others. . . . "[5]

In this way alone, by standing on the level of every brother and sister, in this way alone can you share the hungers of the human family; in this way alone can you be the servant of all.

Third, death. I don't mean simply your ultimate dying. I mean, more immediately, the daily dying to yourself that is inescapable in Christian living. I mean the dying that stems from openness to God and self-emptying. To die to yourself is to live to God and to others. In my experience, that sort of dying makes two demands on you. (1) You come to your brothers and sisters accepting your own brokenness. Not fearless and tearless, not unscarred and unshaken. Quite the contrary; you are a wounded healer, dreadfully vulnerable. In giving life to others, you die a little each time, each day. (2) You have to destroy the smallness in you, the narrowness that plagues human living—where you are wrapped up in yourself, where all that matters is what you want and what you need, your own little hurts and your secret joys. No, if you are risen with Christ, then, for the love of Christ, live a risen life! Stop massaging the latest bruise to your ego. Think big and love lots. Against all the odds, you will even feel better!

Dear friends in Christ: I assure you, after all too many years, after all too many mistakes, *this* is how you share in the redeeming work of Christ; this is how you bring life, Christ's life, to a hungry world. If the words "obedience," "humiliation," and "death" make you gag, spit them out! I am asking you (1) to be open, (2) to be human, (3) to be big—broken but big. Do that, live like that, and you will bring the joy of Jesus to every face you touch. Live like that and you will not worry how important you are. For to every child of

God you meet you will be able to say in all honesty and Christlike humor: "You know, you're the greatest!"

Dahlgren Chapel
Georgetown University
September 23, 1979

19
PARTYING IN CHRIST
Twenty-eighth Sunday of the Year (A)

- *Isaiah 25:6–10*
- *Philippians 4:12–14, 19–20*
- *Matthew 22:1–14*

Once again the liturgy confronts us with a parable (Mt 22:1–14). And once again there is much to puzzle us, irritate us, make us feel that the whole thing is unreal. Royal wedding invitations to which *all* the invited respond "no." When the king insists, his messengers are killed. The king retaliates: His troops destroy the murderers and burn their city. To fill the dining room, the king pulls in people off the streets, the nice and the not-so-nice. One poor fellow doesn't have a wedding garment; out he goes on his tush. And the whole thing ends with a vague, disturbing warning: "Many are called, but few are chosen" (Mt 22:14). Couldn't the master of parables do better than that?

Before you give up an undigestible banquet for an edible brunch, let me try to spice up the king's dinner. With three courses, of course. First, an appetizer from the Jewish world, to tease your taste. Second, the main dish, quite international—really what the king's dinner is all about. Third, a local dessert, prepared especially for you—possibly a bit tart for some Christian tastes.

I

First, the appetizer. Something a bit startling: The parable you have just heard is really two parables.[1] The first parable (vv. 1–10) ends with the wedding hall filled; and so it ends on a happy note, with the rabble, the ragtag, the riffraff hoisting one to the king and singing the equivalent of "For he's a jolly good fellow." That's the parable of the Great Banquet or Wedding Feast. The second parable is the parable of the Guest without a Wedding Garment, a fellow from the streets who did not find the time or take the trouble to wash his clothes clean. You find this only in Matthew, not in Luke's version (Lk 14:16–24). Luke ends with the house about to be filled with outcasts and underprivileged; the "beautiful people" originally invited have not been killed, but they are not to taste of the banquet. End of parable.

Now why did Matthew take another parable of Jesus, an independent parable, the case of the rejected guest, and insert it here? For an appetizer, let me simply say this. Once the parable of the Great Banquet was applied to the Christian community, it ran the risk of being misunderstood. Did the life of the community have nothing to say to the sinner? Did Jesus' invitation not call for change, for conversion, for clean clothes? Were the baptized free of moral responsibility? The evil were as welcome as the good, and could stay evil? It doesn't matter whether you're good or evil—just eat up? No. The second parable told the community: You don't have to buy a tux, but whatever you wear has to be washed, has to be clean. You have to change.

II

Enough of the appetizer. Now for the main course—cuisine international. What is the king's dinner all about? In a single word, salvation—the salvation of the world. But to grasp what that means, you have to understand the situation in which Matthew wrote his Gospel. Don't think of Matthew lounging at the Sea of Galilee, trying to put down exactly what Jesus had said. No. He was writing for a community in transition, a community in process of change.[2] They were largely Jewish-Christians, Jews converted to Christ. It was about the year 85, somewhere in Palestine or Syria. The community was confused, in tension and conflict, bewildered by false prophets. They had been profoundly affected by the destruction of Jerusalem and the Temple by the Romans. Rooted in Jewish tradition, they had to ask themselves: In the context of postwar Judaism, what does it mean to be a Christian? Are we to continue as a special sect within Judaism? Who are we? They were being persecuted by non-Jews; there was in-house betrayal and hatred; widespread wickedness was causing love to grow cold.

In response to all this, Matthew retold the story of Jesus from his conception till after his resurrection. He stressed four themes for his community. (1) Though originally sent to Israel, you must give yourselves to the wider Gentile mission. (2) You are no longer a sect within Judaism; you have a separate identity. (3) Forgive and love one another, for your mission will fail if you cannot live with your own divisions. (4) When Christ returns, he will judge not only you but the Gentiles to whom you are sent.

Within this historical situation today's parable makes sense. Jesus' own parable was shorter and simpler. He was taking aim only at his opponents and critics: You spurned the invitation to salvation, and so God has called the publicans and sinners. Matthew applies it to the whole mystery of Jews and Gentiles. Now it becomes an allegory of salvation, an outline of God's plan for redemption, from the appearance of the prophets, through the fall of Jerusalem, to the Last Judgment.

The feast, the great evening banquet, is salvation. The first servants sent out are the Old Testament prophets, those men who were called by God to speak in His name, to say "Thus says Yahweh." The guests first invited to the marriage feast of Yahweh's Son are the people of Israel. They reject His call. The second group of messengers are the apostles and missionaries sent by God to Israel. Their message too is rejected; some of them are put to death. The city the king burns is Jerusalem, destroyed in 70. The mission to the streets is God's invitation to the Gentiles: All peoples are now called to the feast of salvation. The entry into the wedding hall is baptism, entry into the community of salvation. The inspection of the guests by the king is the Last Judgment. The "outer darkness" is hell.

III

Now that, my friends, is a very heavy meal. There is indeed much to nourish you there: God's saving care for all of us from ages back. But there is also much to give you heartburn: It seems awfully harsh on the Jews. For easier Christian digestion, therefore, I suggest a local dessert, my own recipe, even though it may prove a trifle tart.

The name of the dish is common enough: community. Remember Matthew's problem? His community was torn: infighting, lack of love, especially the agonizing question of Christian identity: Who are we? Now the world-wide community called Catholic has for two decades been experiencing parallel problems, and many of our local communities are dreadfully divided. At times we Catholic cats claw at one another with a savagery that must make Christ weep. The Eucharist that above all else should make us one in love divides us in cordial dislike. Doctrinally, thanks to theologians in and out of residence, it seems as if everything Catholic is up for grabs. The identity tags are all but gone: novenas on Monday and fish on Friday, the Rosary and Benediction, the wimple and the Roman collar—even confession. Who are we?

A homily is not a dissertation, and so that question will not be argued here. But much that Matthew said to his community he would surely adapt to our situation. First, you do have an identity, a Catholic identity. In part, it is an identity you share with other Christians. With them, you confess Jesus as Lord and Savior; like them, you are united to the Father and to one another through Christ in the Spirit. In part, you are different; for you express your commitment to Christ through a body of beliefs, a system of sacraments, an order of authority that other Christians cannot totally share. Despite our theological battles "religiously" reported in *Time* and *Newsweek,* you should know, and I sense that you do experience, what it means to be a Catholic Christian.[3]

Second, Matthew would say: You have a wider mission than to your own Dahlgren community. The danger in any well-knit group—academic, military, political, social, spiritual—is narcissism: Like the beautiful youth Narcissus in Greek mythology, you risk falling in love with your own reflection. It is indeed an impressive image you project: warm, open, generous, accepting, enthusiastic. You are a community of love, alive with and for one another. In this context you have felt compelled to ask: Is your mission locked into this Georgetown quadrangle? Matthew would answer: Absolutely not! The world is your parish. Where precisely? Thailand or 14th Street? Appalachia or your office? The corridor you live on or the streets you walk? No homilist knows. The encouraging thing is that as a community we have begun to feel uneasy; we sense that, grateful as we are for all our Dahlgren blessings, we may be wrapping them up in Georgetown napkins and clutching them tightly to our happy little bodies.

Third, Matthew would repeat: Whatever your mission is, it will fail if you cannot live with your divisions. The Catholic Church is hurting. Not for the first time; and only those ignorant of history think of today as the nadir, the pits, of Catholic existence. But we do hurt; countless divisions rend us. The point is, the hurts that tear us must be made redemptive. Whether in our tiny chapel or in our diocese (yes, *our* diocese) or in the Church at large, we all have wounds to bind—our own and others': fears and tears, frustration and anger, loneliness and lovelessness, bitterness and envy, even the frightful feeling that in this royal hall I can no longer taste the banquet of salvation.

In a few moments we shall receive one of our own dear young friends into full communion with the Catholic Church, full communion with our community. What she has tasted of the King's dinner she apparently likes; her reaction to the rest of the feast I dare not predict. Much depends on the rest of the guests—how well, how lovingly, how joyfully you and I party in Christ.

Dahlgren Chapel
Georgetown University
October 11, 1981

20
I GIVE THEE THANKS, O LORD
Twenty-eighth Sunday of the Year (C)

- *2 Kings 5:14–17*
- *2 Timothy 2:8–13*
- *Luke 17:11–19*

Several weeks ago I heard a striking story. Of old there was a tyrannical king, all-powerful. He was able to work his will on his subjects in all things. All things save one: He was unable to destroy their belief in God. So he summoned his three wisest counselors. "Tell me," he said. "Where can I hide this people's God so that they will not be able to find Him?" Said the first wise man: "Hide their God beyond the farthest star; there they will not find Him." "Not so," said the second wise man. "One day these people may discover how to fly beyond the stars; that day they will find their God. Rather, hide Him on the floor of the sea." "No," said the third wise man. "One day these people may learn how to swim to the bottom of the ocean; that day they will find their God. Rather, hide Him in the everyday lives of the people; there no one will ever find Him."

Hide God in the everyday lives of the people. I thought of that story when I was mulling over the ten lepers healed, mulling over the one who returned to thank the healer, mulling over the plaint of Jesus: "Was no one found to return and give praise to God except this foreigner?" (Lk 17:18). Three quick ideas. First, what lies behind all this biblical talk about thanking and praising? Second, how ought a Christian to express thanks, praise God? And third, what does the story of the lepers say to our everyday lives?

126

I

First then, a word from God's word.[1] In the Bible, thanks and praise go hand in hand. Thanksgiving is a response. To what? To God's self-revealing, His mighty deeds in creation, His ceaseless gifts to His people, His particular kindness to each frail human. Thanksgiving stems from a joyful discovery of God's greatness and glory, an intense awareness of God's gifts, a sense of wonder in the face of God's generosity. It is a public confession of who God is and what He has done. Thanksgiving runs through so many of the Psalms:

> I give thee thanks, O Lord, with all my heart;
>   before the gods I sing thy praise;
> I bow down before thy holy temple
>   and give thanks to thy name for thy
>   steadfast love and thy faithfulness;
> for thou hast exalted above everything
>   thy name and thy word.
> On the day I called, thou didst answer me,
>   my strength of soul thou didst increase.
> All the kings of the earth shall praise thee, O Lord,
>   for they have heard the words of thy mouth;
> and they shall sing of the ways of the Lord,
>   for great is the glory of the Lord. . . .
> Though I walk in the midst of trouble,
>   thou dost preserve my life. . . .
> The Lord will fulfil His purpose for me;
>   thy steadfast love, O Lord, endures for ever. . . .
>
>   (Ps 138)

If there is any difference between thanksgiving and praise, it lies in this: Praise looks more to God Himself than to His gifts. It is closer to adoration; I am ecstatic, "out of" myself, lost in God. I sing of God simply because He is God. And so the Psalmist sings:

> Praise the Lord!
> Praise, O servants of the Lord,
>   praise the name of the Lord!
> Blessed be the name of the Lord
>   from this time forth and for evermore!
> From the rising of the sun to its setting
>   the name of the Lord is to be praised!

> The Lord is high above all nations,
> and His glory above the heavens!
> (Ps 112:1–4)

The New Testament builds on the Old. In the new covenant, thanksgiving is inseparable from praise, from glorification, from confession, from blessing. But something new has been added. Christian thanksgiving is a response to the grace given by God in Jesus Christ. The object of thanksgiving, through all sorts of happenings and signs, remains ever the same: the mystery of Christ. And so the mother of Jesus sings her Magnificat: "My soul magnifies the Lord . . . for He who is mighty has done great things for me" (Lk 1:46, 49). The father of the Baptist shouts his Benedictus: "Blessed be the Lord God of Israel, for He has visited and redeemed His people" (Lk 1:68). Jesus rejoices in the Holy Spirit: "I thank thee, Father, Lord of heaven and earth, that thou hast hidden these things from the wise and understanding and revealed them to the childlike and innocent" (Lk 10:21). And Paul proclaims his striking thanksgiving to the Ephesians:

> Blessed be the God and Father of our Lord Jesus Christ, who has blessed us in Christ with every spiritual blessing in the heavenly places, even as He chose us in him before the foundation of the world, that we should be holy and blameless before him in love. He destined us to be His sons and daughters through Jesus Christ . . . to the praise of His glorious grace which He freely bestowed on us in the Beloved. In him we have redemption through his blood, the forgiveness of our trespasses. . . . For He has made known to us in all wisdom and insight the mystery of His will, according to His purpose which He set forth in Christ as a plan for the fulness of time, to unite all things in him.
> In him . . . we who first hoped in Christ have been destined and appointed to live for the praise of his glory. In him you also, who have heard the word of truth, the gospel of your salvation, and have believed in him, were sealed with the promised Holy Spirit, which is the guarantee of our inheritance until we acquire possession of it, to the praise of His glory.
> (Eph 1:3–14)

Our thanksgiving *is* Jesus Christ. This emerges thrillingly from the special New Testament word for thanksgiving: *eucharisteō, eu-*

charistia. Christian thanksgiving is eucharist, and its perfect expression is the sacramental Eucharist, the thanksgiving of the Lord given by him to his Church. Jesus' whole life is one long act of thanksgiving, one undivided eucharist—begun in Bethlehem, supremely symbolized at the Last Supper, carried to consummation on the cross. That same thanksgiving is now our Christian existence, from birth to death: "Through him, and with him, and in him" our hearts and voices give praise and glory to God our Father.

II

This leads logically to my second point: How ought a Christian to express thanks, praise God? Jesus told us vividly how *not* to thank God. You remember the Pharisee praying in the temple: "God, I thank thee that I am not like other men, extortioners, unjust, adulterers, or even like this tax collector. I fast twice a week, I give tithes of all that I get" (Lk 18:11–12). Now Jesus did not accuse the Pharisee of injustice or adultery. Jesus did not deny that the Pharisee fasted on Mondays and Thursdays, gave a tenth of his income to religion and the poor. The problem lay rather in his heart: He trusted in himself and he despised others (Lk 18:9). This is not to bless God; this is not to give God the glory; this is not to thank God—except to thank Him for making me different.

This attitude is poles apart from that of Thomas Merton. He describes a shattering, liberating experience. He had been a monk for sixteen or seventeen years. Walking through the shopping district of Louisville, he suddenly felt that he was waking from a dream. A dream that he was somehow separate, isolated in a special world; the illusion that by taking vows monks become a different species of being. Yes indeed, the monk belongs to God; but, as Merton put it, "so does everybody else belong to God. We just happen to be conscious of it, and to make a profession out of this consciousness. But does that entitle us to consider ourselves different, or even *better,* than others? The whole idea is preposterous." Then follows a splendid, shivering outburst:

> This sense of liberation from an illusory difference was such a relief and such a joy that I almost laughed out loud. And I suppose my happiness could have taken form in the words: "Thank

God, thank God that I *am* like other men, that I am only a man among others." . . . It is a glorious destiny to be a member of the human race, though it is a race dedicated to many absurdities and one which makes many terrible mistakes: yet, with all that, God Himself gloried in becoming a member of the human race![2]

How ought we Christians to express thanks? By praising God for two breath-taking gifts. First, He has made us what we are, men and women of flesh and spirit, men and women fashioned in His own image. Second, God thought so much of what we are that He *became* what we are, bone of our bones, flesh of our flesh. In the lovely couplet of the English poet John Donne:

'Twas much, that man was made like God before,
But, that God should be made like man, much more.[3]

III

Which brings me to my third question: What does the Gospel story of the ten lepers say to our everyday lives? I shall not waste time beating on the nine no-shows: "Where are the nine?" (Lk 17:17). I shall not suggest that they were ungrateful. Perhaps they were hugging dear ones for the first time in years, or hoisting a few at the local pub. Nor am I interested in thanksgiving for special occasions, for major or minor miracles. I'm sure that, if you are cured of cataracts or prostate cancer, you will sprint posthaste to the crucifix.

But the issue is not, how thankful are you at critical moments? The issue is rather, is your life a ceaseless eucharist? Biblical thanksgiving, I said, is a response: a response to God's self-revealing, His mighty deeds in history, His gifts to His people, His kindness to each man and woman. Now this presence of God, this action of God, never ceases. He is always here, He is always active—in the world, in the Church, in us. And so our response—discovery, awareness, wonder, confession—must itself be a ceaseless thing. Otherwise God will indeed be a hidden God, hidden in the rut and routine, in the insensitivity and unawareness, of our daily lives.

The point is, our *lives* must be our response, our thanksgiving, our praise, our confession. God's basic gift to you is simply . . . you.

Then, by God, praise God by accepting yourself! Thank God you are this unique man, this unique woman! Not perfect by any means; small and selfish and sinful; terribly vulnerable without Right Guard, and unable to rely on Rely. And still you are unique, shaped by God's love into the singular creature that is you. Thank God, with the Psalmist, for the wonder of yourself (Ps 139:13–15)!

With the gift that is you, God has given . . . Himself. This spirit of yours is not just a repository of fears and anxieties; this flesh of yours is not just a foaming barrel of Schlitz. You are a temple of God, a living shrine where Father, Son, and Spirit dwell, a tabernacle dearer to God than the tabernacle before you. Then, by God, praise God by living like a shrine of God! Oh, not eyes cast down, not hands ever folded. Simply by acting as anyone would who feels God in him, God pulsing within her.

With the gift that is you and with the gift that is Himself, God has given you . . . others. It is an incredible gift. You are not alone, not an island. You have someone else to feast your eyes on; you have the music of another voice; you can feel another's touch in love. Then, by God, praise God by giving yourself to others! Let others see *you,* hear *your* dulcet tones; reach out yourself to those who need your weakness as well as your strength, your trembling as well as your courage, your passion and your compassion.

Only thus will you reveal God in your everyday lives, make each moment a thanksgiving, a eucharist without words. Only then will this sacramental Eucharist lose its "Sunday only" look, gather up the whole week, the rest of your living, in a supreme "thank you" that offers to the Father not only the body of Christ but your own body as well.

Let me leave each of you with an uncharitable question that goes back to my opening story. If a man or a woman were searching for God, would that man or woman find Him in your everyday life?

Dahlgren Chapel
Georgetown University
October 12, 1980

21
EVEN A LONELY VOICE
Thirtieth Sunday of the Year (B)

- *Jeremiah 31:7–9*
- *Hebrews 5:1–6*
- *Mark 10:46–52*

Tuesday night, October fourth, an old black woman stood in a crowd on 141st Street in Harlem. She had been standing on that street for seven long hours, waiting in patience and anticipation for one person to pass by. Later that night, after Pope John Paul II had disappeared into the night, she stood alone on that same street, smiling as tears rolled down her cheeks. A lifelong Baptist, she said in rapture: "I touched him. I seen misery and I seen hard times. But see me now, this night I'm crying 'bout the most exciting thing that ever happened to me."[1]

Today, dear friends, I want to talk about a fact of life inspired by that touching Harlem scene and by the liturgical readings that have been proclaimed to you. I want to talk about . . . taking the initiative in loving. As usual, three points: God's initiative, a pope's initiative, your initiative.

I

First, God's initiative. Here the liturgical readings are rich. Jeremiah tells (Jer 31:7–9) how God will end the Babylonian exile, restore all Israel, assemble the dispersed in their homeland. The material civilization will be recovered; the political community will be reinstated; its king will be the perfect intermediary between Yahweh and His people. *God* will do this. And He will do it with compassion: "Among [those gathered from the farthest parts of

132

the earth will be] the blind and the lame, the woman with child and [she] who is in travail. . . . With weeping they shall come, and with consolations I will lead them back . . . for I am a father to Israel, and Ephraim is my first-born" (Jer 31:8–9).

The Letter to the Hebrews makes the same point in a different context. Whether it is the Jewish high priest or the new high priest Christ, their ministry ultimately goes back to God's own choosing. To human compassion must be added divine appointment (Heb 5:1–6). That much is basic to any and every theology of ministry, whether nurtured on the banks of the Tiber or on the shores of the Potomac. Whoever is called to serve, it is God who calls; God takes the initiative.

The blind beggar by the Jericho roadside (Mk 10:46–52) might seem an exception. After all, isn't it he who calls out "Jesus, son of David, have mercy on me!" (v. 47)? Isn't it he who makes the first move? Only on the face of it, on the surface of things. God took the initiative, the initiative in loving him, in at least three ways, at three points. God loved him from eternity and at a moment in time fashioned him from his mother's flesh. God sent His only Son in the beggar's skin to save him from his sins. And God made it possible for him to believe, made it possible for him to cry out to Jesus; for "your faith has made you well" (v. 52), and faith is a gift. Unless God had first loved him, the beggar could not have loved in return. Unless God had come to him, he could not have come to God. If we but turn to God, Augustine insisted, that is itself a gift of God. God always takes the initiative; God is always first in loving; God first comes to us.

II

Second, a pope's initiative. Earlier this month you and I and much of America experienced a unique initiative. Fourteen years ago Paul VI came to the U.N.; three weeks ago John Paul II came to *us*. Oh, we may argue for months—and we will—on details of the message he brought, from migrant workers to religious habits, from consumerism to contraception, from the rights of "man" to woman priests. But over and above any individual message, the essential message he brought was himself. It may well be that the heart of his visit was summed up in his chant to the young: "John Paul Two—he loves you!"

The point is, he did not wait for us to come to him, to ask an audience. He came to us; and he came with love. In Madison Square Garden he beckoned to a little girl; instantly she "was swept off her feet, handed gently upward from a joyous crowd of 20,000 school children . . . finally reaching his loving hands. He embraced her as his own and, for a few moments, placed her above him on the top of his truck."[2] He wiped the sweat from the face of a priest who had conducted the choir at St. Patrick's Cathedral. He sang gospel music with blacks on the streets of Harlem. He accepted gifts from America's youth: blue jeans, a guitar, a T-shirt with a Big Apple slogan (*Time* called it "a boisterous love-in"[3]). He came to Boston's Italians, to New York's blacks, to Chicago's Hispanics. He came to cathedral and stadium, to university and ghetto, to skyscraper and farmland, to White House and whitewashed church, to the powerful at the U.N. and the handicapped in D.C. And wherever he went, his arms were tirelessly outstretched; everywhere he pressed flesh with tough but gentle hands; every gesture said "I love you."

The point is, *he* came to *us,* and he came with love. And in coming, a columnist wrote, "He has brought us back to elemental things, and shown that even a lonely voice, crying for the beliefs we have lost, can be important."[4]

III

Even a lonely voice can be important. This leads into my third point: your initiative. You see, you cannot leave the initiative in loving to God and pope. God's initiative, in creating and re-creating us, is indeed indispensable; and John Paul's initiative was a unique type of love-witness. But those initiatives are insufficient of themselves; they can be lost without your "lonely voice." God's face is hidden, and His vicar has gone home.

Through almost a year I have grown to know this community of ours and to love it. I am amazed how open you are to one another, how responsive to needs—the needs of 12:15 Christians and so many others outside this sanctuary. I am impressed and delighted.

But it is one thing to be responsive, another thing to take the initiative. I dare not wait on my tight little island until an SOS reaches me; I may not lounge comfortably in my little cell until someone knocks. John Paul II said sadly in Harlem: "How many people have never known joy! They live in our neighborhoods, they have never met a brother or sister who touched their lives with the love of Jesus." I dare not wait for them to come to me, to beg like Lazarus for the crumbs of love that fall from my table. Too many are embarrassed, or shy, or afraid, or locked into themselves. They cry inside, but I will not hear that cry unless I make the first move.

I am asking you to go out to people. A Jesuit I know in Cincinnati visits three hospitals each night—one Catholic, one Jewish, one Protestant—after a full day's work. Father Horace McKenna of St. Aloysius started a housing project and a soup kitchen, seeks out the lonely and the unloved, the destitute and the despairing. Georgetown students fly to India, give a year of their lives to the outcasts of society; soon six will travel to refugee resettlement camps in the United States and abroad. An aunt of mine, even in her seventies, made her aching way to every Polish wake within striking distance of Bay Ridge, Brooklyn.

These are a few homespun examples from a bottomless bag of Christian initiatives. I recall them because I want to challenge you—you who are blessed with so much: eyes that open on beauty, ears that thrill to music, minds that drink in knowledge, hands that touch in love, stomachs that grow fat even on Georgetown food. Daniel Berrigan claims: "Churchgoers in America are used to lukewarm yogurt." I refuse to feed you yogurt. I should like you to leave this chapel disturbed, restless, dissatisfied—not because the choir did not sing your song, not because miming the Gospel isn't your "thing," not because the homilist is a beastly bore with three points, but disturbed because, for all your generosity, you are not as forward in loving as God wants you to be.

"Take heart," the Gospel proclaims today, "he is calling you" (Mk 10:49). Jesus is calling you—not only those who today have been commissioned as readers, ushers, acolytes, sacristans, liturgical artists, or Eucharistic ministers. You. Each of you. And when Jesus asks you what you want of him, say with the blind beggar: "Master, let me see" (Mk 10:51). Lord, let me look for "lost horizons." Let my eyes open not only on beauty but on ugliness, on the poor and the powerless, on the ailing and the aged, on the hatred that eats away at human hearts. Let me see where I can love without limit, without measure or calculation. Not some fluffy, gossamer kind of loving. No, to be genuinely Christian, I must be like you in loving. But you loved even unto crucifixion. So, let me experience the kind of love where loving will make me retch, scream in pain, want to run away.

Dear friends in Christ: I am asking you—better still, our Lord is asking you—not simply to return love for love. He asks you to take the lead in loving. Mother Teresa should not be today's *extraordinary* Christian. This is our ceaseless tradition, from the gray day the Son of God mounted a cross for us without our even asking it. Blind beggars all, let us beg the Master today, now, simply to let us see.

Dahlgren Chapel
Georgetown University
October 28, 1979

22
ONLY IF YOU RISK
Thirty-third Sunday of the Year (A)

- *Proverbs 31:10–13, 19–20, 30–31*
- *1 Thessalonians 5:1–6*
- *Matthew 25:14–30*

With three fascinating readings, there are three possibilities for a homily. I could regale you with the ideal wife of Proverbs (Prov 31:10–31): more precious than Tiffany's best, trusted by her husband and blessed by her children, in her mouth wisdom and laughter, a combination of housewife and businesswoman, openhanded to the poor and needy. But I shall not; for, as a genial Jesuit used to confess, "I'm a brave man but not a hero."

I could speculate about the thief in Thessalonians (1 Thess 5:1–6). I mean "the day of the Lord," which will come upon you suddenly and destructively unless you are awake and sober. But I shall not; for I know as little about the Lord's second coming as I do about women.

That leaves the Gospel (Mt 25:14–30), that intriguing story of three servants and what they did with the money their master entrusted to them: five thousand dollars, two thousand, and one thousand. I want to focus on the third fellow—a man of modest ability who would not trade with his master's money but buried it in the ground. And what I want to talk about is precisely what this servant did not do: I want to talk about risk. I shall begin with a recent risk, go back to the cautious servant, and end with you.

I

First, the recent risk. Last month I was privileged to preach in this chapel at a University memorial Mass.[1] The Mass paid tribute to a remarkable Muslim. A Muslim whose roots were in revolution, but who renounced violence. A man who was ready to risk—to risk everything for peace. Literally everything. He risked his friendships; he risked his country; he risked his life. And the life he risked he lost; the warmakers killed him.

Was the risk worth it? In one sense we do not know, we cannot say. It may be that Sadat's death is the death of hope in the Middle East, that his risk is sheer tragedy, that it was all for naught. After all, at the news of his death millions of his fellow Arabs laughed in the streets; there was a satisfied roar from the Russian bear; war may still destroy Sadat's dream.

Only time will tell whether the Egyptian's risk was effective of peace, and in that sense worth his blood. But even if peace does not bless the Middle East, the risk he took is admirable. Someone had to do something, break the deadlock, capture the free world's imagination. And so, not knowing what lay before him, knowing only that what lay behind was riskier still, he took a chance, one giant step to the City of Peace.

II

Second, the case of the cautious servant. He was apparently a decent chap; otherwise his master would hardly have entrusted him with a thousand dollars. But not the smartest of the three servants; each was given money "according to his ability" (v. 15), and he got the least. Servants 1 and 2 were shrewd operators; they bulled the market, doubled their investment. Not so servant 3. He was afraid—afraid because his master was a grasping man who liked his money, "a hard man" (v. 24) who did not look kindly on failure. Lose that thousand and, man, you're in deep trouble! What to do? Only one alternative: Keep it safe, don't take any chances. So he buried the money. According to rabbinical law, burying was the best security against theft. If you buried a pledge or a deposit immediately upon receiving it, you were no longer liable; you did not have to make restitution if it was stolen.

Servant 3 buried his master's money. He played it safe—or so he thought. No risk, none whatsoever—or so he thought. The trouble was, he underestimated his master. The master was painfully honest with him: "You knew what I was like; you knew how I react when money is involved. So why didn't you bank the money? I would at least have had interest when I returned" (cf. vv. 26–27).

As a perceptive commentator has put it, "In the fear of the one-talent man we see the anxiety of one who will not step into the unknown. He will not risk trying to fulfill his own possibilities; therefore, his existence is circumscribed in the narrowest kind of way. Action is paralyzed by anxiety, and the self of our protagonist is only a shadow of what it potentially is."[2] The servant blames someone else, his hard master, for his own failure, his lack of responsibility. The final tragedy? What was given to him is now taken away: "Take the talent from him" (v. 28). He no longer has the chance to act responsibly, to risk. The tragic movement has three stages. (1) The servant refused to risk; (2) he projected his guilt onto his master; (3) he lost any possibility of living meaningfully in this world.[3]

III

Sadat risked, the servant refused to risk. So what? Where does that leave you and me? How do we move from Egypt and Palestine to the District of Columbia? Let me risk a rapid reflection.

The name of the game is risk. The whole human bag is a risk. If you don't know that, you've been living on Cloud Nine. In the measure that you are really alive, you are risking; for you take all sorts of chances without knowing how they will come out. To marry is to risk: You surrender your private self to a community of selves, risk your individual life in the hope of finding it more fully with another; and today the odds are only 50–50. To love is to risk: You open yourself to all the burden that being loved lays on you; and uncounted men and women crumble under it. To be a top-flight doctor or lawyer, to be in politics or business, is a risk: You may end up terribly narrow and one-sided, closed to everything save a spastic colon or a court case, public applause or private enterprise. To be a priest is to risk: Too many of us are crotchety, peevish, self-centered bachelors incapable of loving or being loved. Simply to be free is to risk: You can say no to God, betray your dearest friend with a kiss. In a word, to live humanly is to launch out into a large unknown.

But my focus here is that particular human risk which is the Christian risk. To begin with, you commit yourself to a Christ you cannot see. Your act of faith is a breath-taking risk. You not only affirm truths with your intellect: God is One and Three; the Son of God took flesh and died for you; you will rise from death and live without end. You surrender your whole person to God in Christ: "To you I offer myself—all I am and all I hope to be."

But here you have left the secure world of philosophical proof and scientific demonstration; here you do violence to what you see and hear, touch and smell and taste. You see a criminal on a cross, and you cry "My Lord and my God!" You hear words from a book, and they turn for you into the word of God. You touch a hand in love, and you sense the presence of Christ. You smell incense, and the Lord pervades your space. You taste bread, and you eat the body of Christ.

Risk? Of course! Because you do not have certainty and *then* commit yourself to God in Christ; you must first commit yourself in order to have any assurance at all. Risk because faith is not nice thoughts and feelings; it determines your life, who you are and what you do. Abraham was commanded to sacrifice his son Isaac. Esther risked death for her Jewish brothers and sisters: "I will go to the king, though it is against the law; and if I perish, I perish" (Esth 4:16). Committed to crucifixion, Jesus did not suspect he would beg his Father to remove this bitter cup if at all possible. When Thomas More became chancellor of England, who could predict that one day "the king's good servant" would pay with his head for being "God's [servant] first"? Those who give up literally everything to follow the naked Christ naked—from Antony and Francis to Teresa of Avila and Teresa of Calcutta—do not know what tomorrow will bring. Ignatius Loyola did not know what God meant when He promised to show him "favor" in Rome: "Perhaps I shall be crucified." And we smaller folk, we too risk a cross if we live our Christian commitment. We know a cross will be there; the risk is, we do not know what shape it will take.

If we risk in committing ourselves to a Christ we cannot see, we risk perhaps more in committing ourselves to a Church we can see. For this is a pilgrim Church, a community on the way, not yet there; a body of sinful men and women, at times in startling contradiction to the Lord who heads it, to the Spirit who gives it life. Its outward face is not only spotted and wrinkled; it constantly changes—from a stone altar to a wooden table, from Aramaic to Greek and Latin and English, from stony silence to squeals of peace, from Gregorian to guitar, from an all-male ministry to women in the sanctuary, from unquestioning obedience to strident resistance, from the simple confusion of the first Pentecost to the complexities of a new code of law.

And still it is Christ's community; here is where he expects us to experience him. And not only to endure it but to love it, to take it for better or worse, for richer or poorer, in sickness and in health, until death. Otherwise we are no different from the cautious servant. First, we play it safe, hedge our bets, stay out of trouble, live our secure Christianity and don't get involved: Let the kooks take care of starving Cambodians or make the Dahlgren gestures at the Our Father. Second, when things get tough, we lay the blame on someone else: a harsh pastor, a Roman document on birth control, paranoid nuns in parochial schools, uninspired liturgy, marriage laws, priests in politics, Catholics who go piously to church but don't live it—the thousand and one reasons that keep us from looking within ourselves. We are victims; someone else is responsible for our failure. Third, we can indeed feel free, free of responsibility; we no longer have to do anything with our "talent." But the freedom can be an illusion. Without responsibility, there is no Christian freedom.

My sisters and brothers: To be a disciple of Christ, you have to lose your life in order to find it. I do not know what life it is that Christ is asking you to surrender; wire-tapping is illegal even for Jesuits. I do know there are special moments, critical moments, in every life where to be Christian you have to choose, commit yourself, risk. The Danish philosopher-theologian Kierkegaard put it simply yet profoundly. He saw three possible attitudes you can have with respect to your self: aesthetic, ethical, religious. The aesthetic: You refuse to commit yourself to anything permanent—it limits your possibilities; and so you drift from one pleasure to another. The ethical: You do choose, you do commit yourself, you accept the limitations that choice imposes, and in this way you become a real person. The religious: You make this choice in dependence on God—the only way in which your freedom can overcome its native insufficiency; only in faith is freedom made free. Which is your attitude? Who are you?

The encouraging thing is, *our* Master is not a hard master. But you won't know that his "yoke is easy" and his "burden light" (Mt 11:30) just by reading the Gospels: He sounds terribly demanding, expects an accounting, threatens "exterior darkness" (Mt 25:30). You will only experience how "gentle" (Mt 11:29) he is if you let go, if you surrender yourself, if you say trustingly "Into your hands I commit my spirit" (Lk 23:46). Only if you risk.

Dahlgren Chapel
Georgetown University
November 15, 1981

23
I NEVER STOP THANKING GOD
Thirty-third Sunday of the Year (B)

- *Daniel 12:1–3*
- *1 Corinthians 1:3–9*
- *Mark 13:24–32*

For those who like their liturgies simple, today's celebration might seem a bit much. Daniel and Mark move our minds to the end of time; St. Paul directs our thinking to next Thursday's Thanksgiving; on and around our altar we have heaped the fruits of the earth; and all the while a whole people is starving to extinction in Southeast Asia. Overload? Perhaps. And still, I suggest, it all fits together. One key word links all the disparate elements: harvest. Let's see how it might all work together unto our good.

I

First, there is the ultimate harvest. Today's readings from Daniel and Mark lead liturgically to the end of the Church year, to next Sunday's feast, to Christ the King, when the whole of creation will be subjected to the Lord of heaven and earth, when Jesus Christ will be all in all.

Daniel, in a magnificent conclusion to a vision given him by an angel, predicts briefly what will happen at the end of time (Dan 12:1–3). The passage raises more problems than it answers; these three verses have vexed scholars for generations. But this much at least can be drawn from Daniel: At the end of time, an end prefaced by monumental tribulation, the just will find life, sinners will experience only death.[1] In a grand manifestation of Yahweh's power and of His just direction of the world, His faithful servants shall rise to life eternal, the rest "shall awake . . . to shame and everlasting contempt" (v. 2). The wise "shall shine like the brightness of the firmament; and those who turn many to righteousness, like the stars for ever and ever" (v. 3). For the first time we have a clear affirmation that the dead will rise.[2]

The reading from Mark could be Daniel again, with more detail (Mk 13:24–32; see also Dan 7:13). The Son of Man will come "with great power and glory" (v. 26). Before he comes, there will be great "tribulation"; after that "the sun will be darkened, and the moon will not give its light, and the stars will be falling from heaven, and the powers in the heavens will be shaken" (vv. 24–25). But when he comes, he will "gather his elect from the four winds, from the ends of the earth to the ends of heaven" (v. 27).

Yes, dear Christians, there will be a final harvest. (If you're from Texas, you might prefer to call it the last roundup.) It is the new heaven and the new earth predicted by Isaiah (Isa 65:17; 66:22), foreseen in vision by John (Rev 21:1), when all creation will be renewed, freed from imperfection, transformed by God's glory; when earth will no longer be raped or spirit ravaged; when man and woman, from Eden's first pair to the last of blood and bone, will stand rapturously before God in transfigured flesh; when all our pride and prejudice, our passion and pain, our loves and hates, our hopes and fears, our strength and frailty, all our questing and discovering will be harvested by God, and we will be finally fashioned in the image shape of His Son. As John has it, "when he appears, we shall be like him, for we shall see him as he is" (1 Jn 3:2).

II

In the second place, there is today's harvest. That harvest is symbolized by the fruits of the earth we have heaped on and around our altar. There are leaves and flowers; there are apples and nuts, squash and corn; there might even be some spinach around. And in a few short moments there will be bread and wine.

Now this outpouring speaks to us of a rich harvest. It tells us that we have made the *earth* to fructify; to some extent we have subjugated the earth, bent it to our will. We have milked it of oil and mined its diamonds; we split its atoms and harness its energy; from it we shape a drug for healing and a missile for destruction; we eat of it and dress from it; we turn deserts into fertile plains and we make footprints on the moon. And for the fruits of the earth we must, in the words of St. Paul, "never stop thanking God" (1 Cor 1:4). Not indeed for everything we have done with the earth, not for the rape and pillage. But surely we can never stop thanking God for harvests that make it possible to live and to love.

But the fruits on our altar should speak to us of a still richer harvest. "I never stop thanking God," Paul proclaims, "for all the graces you have received through Jesus Christ" (v. 4). This is your richest harvest: *who you are,* what God has made of you through Christ, the gifts of the Spirit that are so opulently yours. And do not tell me that you are poor in the Spirit. Look inside yourself. You have the two gifts Paul begged for the Christians of Corinth: "grace and peace" (v. 3). Grace is the gracious care, the undeserved favor, which God shows to those He has saved in Christ. More basically, grace is God: God above you, God around you, God within you. Peace includes so much: Your sins have been forgiven, you have been reconciled to God, you live in love with your brothers and sisters. These are the basic blessings of Christianity, and they can come only from God. And they are yours.

More than that: Paul says "you have been enriched in so many ways" (v. 5). Only you know how many. Some strike me quickly: Christ has revealed himself to you; you have died and risen with him; you listen to his word, pillow him on your tongue; you touch his love to others. Paul has told you what the fruits of the Spirit are: "love, joy, peace, patience, kindness, goodness, faithfulness, gentleness, self-control" (Gal 5:22–23). These indeed you enjoy. Perhaps not always, not without some "works of the flesh" (Gal 5:19); but on the whole you are led by the Spirit. Yes, there is trouble and tribulation; for you live your Christianness in the shadow of a cross. And still you are a temple of the Holy Spirit; still you should rejoice with a joy no man or woman can take from you. You are now, at this moment, first fruits of the risen Christ; you are the earnest, the pledge, of the glorious harvest to come. "You will not be without any of the gifts of the Spirit while you are waiting for our Lord Jesus Christ to be revealed" (1 Cor 1:7).

III

And yet, our joy in these harvests, the music in our hearts, must be muted. Muted by the millions for whom there is no harvest save hunger; who have no thanks to give, save for a quick death. I see an Associated Press photograph: "a Cambodian mother holding in her arms the rigid body of her dead child . . . Madonna and Pietà in one; here, neither a laughing infant nor a dead man; here, a life not lived, but gone."[3] In four years four million Cambodians have died—half the nation; and in the next few months two and a quarter million more may starve to death. Where is their harvest?

Oh yes, much is being done—by the Red Cross, by UNICEF, by the U.S., by Catholic Relief Services. Soon, I hope, twenty GU doctors will fly to Thailand, twenty GU medical students, a small army of nurses and staff. But the need is mind-boggling, political obstruction overwhelming. Each day a hundred or a thousand Cambodians stumble into Thailand "on reed-thin legs . . . a grisly cavalcade of specters, wrapped in black rags. Many are in the last stages of malnutrition, or are ravaged by . . . dysentery, tuberculosis and malaria. Perhaps the most pathetic images of all are those of tearful, exhausted mothers cradling hollow-eyed children with death's-head faces, their bellies swollen, their limbs as thin and fragile as dried twigs."[4] Where is their harvest?

I have no panacea for Cambodia, no answer to mass starvation, no cure for genocide. Haunted by the Second Holocaust, I choke on my own rhetoric; I have so little to say, no word of hope, no "third point." What Christian counsel dare I give?

The hellish harvest that is Cambodia may well be a graced moment for us, a moment when we must challenge our Christianness. Is Thanksgiving a single, isolated day in my year, or do I "never stop thanking God for all the graces [I] have received through Jesus Christ"? Is this Eucharistic table a private party for me and my friends, or has the Bread of Life transformed me into a eucharist, a thank offering, for the life of the world? How much of my day is waste, not only of food but of talent and time, not only good beer but rich grace? Are others around me starving for attention and affection, for a smile or a touch, because I am small, self-centered, clannish, a tidy package of self-pity? What frontiers must the tearful cross, what walls must the wounded scale, to find hope and healing in me?

Yesterday, in connection with Cambodia, I found myself reading St. Paul's unforgettable vision in the night: "A man of Macedonia was standing beseeching him and saying, 'Come over to Macedonia and help us.' And when he had seen the vision, immediately [he] sought to go on into Macedonia, concluding that God had called [him] ..." (Acts 16:9–10). At that moment I had a frightening fantasy. The Jesus of Matthew's Last Judgment was saying to me reproachfully: "I was hungry and you gave me no food" (Mt 25:42). I protested: "Lord, I couldn't get to Cambodia. It's so far away, and anyhow they wouldn't have let me in." Jesus looked at me sadly and said: "You didn't have to go to Cambodia. All you had to do was cross the street."

Dahlgren Chapel
Georgetown University
November 18, 1979

24

TOY FOR THEOLOGIANS
OR JOY FOR BELIEVERS?
Feast of the Holy Trinity (A)

- *Exodus 34:4–6, 8–9*
- *2 Corinthians 13:11–13*
- *John 3:16–18*

Today's feast sounds tailor-made for a homilist with a flair for three points. Father, Son, and Holy Spirit—what more could I ask? A word of wisdom on each Person, illustrate it with the legend of St. Patrick and the shamrock, and out you trinitarians go, fortified afresh to meet a disbelieving or unitarian world.

It's not quite so simple. Throughout my priestly life (forty years this month) I've been peppered with a persistent complaint: The Trinity says nothing to our daily living. Oh, it may well be true, but it doesn't touch our human or Christian existence. The Trinity is a toy for theologians to play with; it might even keep them from the grosser occasions of sin.

My own thesis is exactly the opposite: The Trinity is highly important for your day-to-day living. Not to save you from hell, but because without the Trinity Christian life would make little sense. The Trinity tells us something remarkable about who we are and what we ought to be. Let me suggest how this is so from three directions, three springboards: the Church, the Bible, and a contemporary poet.

I

First, the view from the Church. The Church's dogma of the Trinity states simply and profoundly: There is but one God. In this

151

one God there are three Persons: Father, Son, and Holy Spirit. These three Persons are really distinct: The Father is not the Son, the Son is not the Father, the Holy Spirit is neither the Father nor the Son. Each of these Persons is really and truly God. And still there is but one God.

A mystery indeed. I mean, we could never have suspected that God is One and Three if God had not told us; and even after He has told us, we cannot explain how this can be. But it is not light for the mind that we seek; it is food for our spirit. And one way of lending meaning to the mystery is to steal St. John's definition of God: "God is Love" (1 Jn 4:8). In the Trinity we find the perfect realization of perfect love; in God's secret life we glimpse the model-without-beginning for every love that has ever begun.[1]

You see, love between persons makes a double demand. Lover and beloved must remain two, yet the two must somehow be one. Love demands distinct persons. Love is we: a you and an I. Whether I love God or another human being, I never cease to be myself. Teresa of Avila, caught up in God, never ceased to be Teresa, never became God. Romeo, forsaking his very name for Juliet, did not become Juliet. Love demands "I" and "thou."

But love forbids "mine" and "thine"—what Augustine calls "those ice-cold words." The two, remaining two, must somehow be one. But we have long since learned a bitter-sweet lesson: Oneness with someone beloved can be achieved only in terms of self-giving. To love is to give—to give of one's self. To love perfectly is to give till there is nothing left to give. Only then do the two, remaining two, become perfectly one.

The marvelous truth about the Trinity is that it is the total realization of perfect love. God's secret is this: There is "I and thou" without "mine and thine." There is "I and thou": There are three Persons. But there is no "mine and thine," no egoism. What makes God God—we call it the divine nature—the Father has it completely, the Son has it completely, the Spirit has it completely. No one has anything the other does not have. The Father gives to the Son literally all that He Himself has, all that makes Him God, all that makes Him Love. And the Son is a perfect Son, because He is the perfect image of His Father. The incredible thing is that the love with which the Son loves the Father is the selfsame infinite love with which the Father loves the Son. And this love of Father and Son, this love *is* the Holy Spirit. God is an eternal exchange of love.

That is why the Trinity is the model-without-beginning for every love that has ever begun. It is the model for our return of love to *God*. Listen again to Augustine: "Are you looking for something to give to God? Give Him yourself." And in the Trinity we find what ought to be our love for *others*. Like the divine Persons, each of whom remains fully Himself, without the Father becoming the Son or the Son becoming the Father, so we too have to be utterly and splendidly ourselves, develop ourselves with all the wealth God has given us. It is the only way we have of being useful to others, by bringing to them, in a gift of ourselves, what we alone can give them. The musical note helps the harmony only by being itself. Love demands "I and thou"; it forbids "mine and thine."

II

Second, the view from the Bible. Scripture has an advantage over dogma: It tells a story. And the story Scripture tells is not God's secret life but God as He breaks into our history, links His life with ours. It tells of a God who fathered children from the dust of the earth, fathered them in His own image and likeness. A Father who never abandoned His children through all their infidelities, who assured them when they felt forsaken and forgotten: "Can a woman forget her sucking child, that she should have no compassion on the son of her womb? Even these may forget, yet I will not forget you" (Isa 49:15). A Father who "so loved the world that He gave His only Son, that whoever believes in Him should not perish but have eternal life" (Jn 3:16).

Scripture tells of a Son divine, equal to the Father, a Son who did not stand on His dignity but emptied Himself of His glory, took on the status of a slave, became like us, humbled Himself with an obedience that climaxed in crucifixion (Phil 2:6–8). A Son who, on the eve of His dying, left you His flesh to eat and His blood to drink. A Son who promised that, if you love Him, His Father will love you and they will make their home in you (Jn 14:23). A Son who pledged that His Father would send you a Counselor to "teach you all things and bring to your remembrance" everything He Himself had said (Jn 14:26).

Scripture tells of a Spirit divine, not isolated in outer space but dwelling within you (1 Cor 3:16). A Spirit that baptizes you into one body, inspires you with different gifts for the benefit of all (1

Cor 12:4–13), teaches you a wisdom not of this world (1 Cor 2:13).
A Spirit whose "fruit . . . is love, joy, peace, patience, kindness,
goodness, faithfulness, gentleness, self-control" (Gal 5:22–23).

What Scripture tells us, in story form, is that the mystery of the
Trinity is our own history: We exist because we are loved—loved
by the Father through the Son in the Spirit. To grasp that, you
need not be Georgetown's theologian in residence; you need only
open yourself in faith to God's word. Read Scripture with eyes of
faith and the Trinity will no longer be a toy for theologians but a
joy for believers. Today you are not simply bent low before mystery. Today is *your* feast—as much your feast as is Christmas or Easter. Today you remember gratefully what makes for Christian
living: You share in the rhythm of God's own life. Christian holiness is essentially trinitarian. Brothers and sisters of Christ, you are
sons and daughters of the Father, precisely because the very Spirit
that is Christ's own is now given to you. And so today you celebrate the Eucharist with singular understanding: Inspired by the
Spirit, you offer Christ (and yourselves) to the Father in sacrifice,
cry aloud in thanksgiving: "Through him, with him, in him, in the
unity of the Holy Spirit, all glory and honor is yours, almighty Father, for ever and ever!"

III

Third, the view from a poet. In 1953 Phyllis McGinley wrote a
perceptive piece of verse entitled "In Praise of Diversity."[2] She recalled that

> Since God invented man, and man
>   At once fell to inventing trouble,
> One virtue, one subversive grace
> Has chiefly vexed the human race.

Her point was: We have ceaselessly felt that there is something
wrong where there is difference, diversity, unlikeness, heterodoxy,
nuance. "There's white, there's black; no tint between . . . now all
must fit one pattern or its opposite." Her answer?

> . . . Yet who would dare
>   Deny that nature planned it other,
> When every freckled thrush can wear

A dapple various from his brother,
When each pale snowflake in the storm
Is false to some imagined norm?

Recalling then what surely was
   The earliest bounty of Creation:
That not a blade among the grass
   But flaunts its difference with elation,
Let us devoutly take no blame
If similar does not mean the same. . . .

Rejoice that under cloud and star
   The planet's more than Maine or Texas.
Bless the delightful fact there are
   Twelve months, nine muses, and two sexes;
And infinite in earth's dominions
Arts, climates, wonders, and opinions. . . .

Praise the disheveled, praise the sleek;
   Austerity and hearts-and-flowers;
People who turn the other cheek
   And extroverts who take cold showers;
Saints we can name a holy day for,
And infidels the saints can pray for.

Praise youth for pulling things apart,
   Toppling the idols, breaking leases;
Then from the upset apple-cart
   Praise oldsters picking up the pieces.
Praise wisdom, hard to be a friend to,
And folly one can condescend to.

Praise what conforms and what is odd,
   Remembering, if the weather worsens
Along the way, that even God
   Is said to be three separate[3] Persons.
Then upright or upon the knee,
Praise Him that by His courtesy,
For all our prejudice and pains,
Diverse His Creation still remains.

Have we plunged from the sublime to the ridiculous? I think
not. With her light touch, the poet has traced one way in which hu-

manity mirrors divinity: We too are one and many. We share a common humanity that makes all men and women brothers and sisters. And still, no one of us is exactly like any other. Each of us is a distinct, unmatchable, unrepeatable, irreplaceable "I." For better or worse, there will never be another Walter J. Burghardt!

Do you want to honor God One and Three? Then "rejoice and be glad" that you are one and many. Rejoice in what you share beneath the skin: the power to know God's creation and love it, to laugh at the human comedy and mourn your mortality, to play merrily and pray heartily, to give of yourself and be given, to live each day and let it go, to share human and divine life. And rejoice in your uniqueness, your difference from one another. Thank God that you are you. Laugh at your personal warts and don't take your gifts too seriously. Know that God loves *you*, not the uplift bra or the Brut that makes you smell like Joe Namath.

It's a great feast, my friends. It's your feast. Today we give glory to God, One and Three; and today we celebrate you, one and many.

Dahlgren Chapel
Georgetown University
June 14, 1981

25
YOU ARE WHAT YOU HAVE RECEIVED
Feast of Corpus Christi (C)

- *Genesis 14:18–20*
- *1 Corinthians 11:23–26*
- *Luke 9:11–17*

Sixteen hundred years ago, a bishop of Jerusalem addressed five instructions during Easter Week to the newly baptized gathered in the Church of the Resurrection. The final lecture dealt with the Eucharistic liturgy. And when the bishop spoke of Communion—the Communion which these fresh converts had received for the first time on the vigil of Easter—he described the rite in these words:

> . . . you hear the chanter inviting you with a sacred melody to communion in the holy mysteries, in the words "O taste and see that the Lord is good" (Ps 33:9). Entrust not the judgment to your bodily palate, but to unwavering faith. For in tasting you taste, not bread and wine, but the antitype of the body and blood of Christ.
>
> When you come up to receive . . . make your left hand a throne for the right (for it is about to receive a King), cup your palm, and so receive the body of Christ; then answer "Amen." Carefully hallow your eyes by the touch of the sacred body, and then partake, taking care to lose no part of it. Such a loss would be like a mutilation of your own body. Why, if you had been given gold dust, would you not take the utmost care to hold it fast, not letting a grain slip through your fingers, lest you be by so much the poorer? How much more carefully, then, will you guard against losing so much as a crumb of that which is more precious than gold or precious stones!

> After partaking of the body of Christ, approach also the chalice of his blood. . . . Bowing low in a posture of worship and reverence as you say "Amen," sanctify yourself by receiving also the blood of Christ. While it is still warm upon your lips, moisten your fingers with it and so sanctify your eyes, your forehead, and other organs of sense. Then wait for the prayer and give thanks to the God who has deigned to admit you to such high mysteries.[1]

Sixteen centuries later, we gather here to do what the Christians of Jerusalem did, what the apostles did in Jerusalem three centuries before that. On this special feast called the Body and Blood of Christ, we shall do what the Lord commanded: "Take and eat. . . . Take and drink." Today, in this chapel, the first century and the fourth and the twentieth come together. The details differ—from the Supper Room through the Church of the Resurrection to Dahlgren Chapel—but the reality is the same. That reality has three facets: first, the basic truth; second, what that truth does to us; third, what that truth demands of us. A word on each.

I

First, the basic truth. It was expressed, simply and profoundly, by Jesus himself: "This is my body. . . . This is my blood" (Mt 26:26, 28). Incredible words, aren't they? Incredible from the first moment our Lord promised it. Do you remember that jolting sentence of Jesus to the Jews: "I say to you, unless you eat the flesh of the Son of Man and drink his blood, you have no life in you" (Jn 6:53)? For many of his disciples this was too much: "This is a hard saying; who can listen to it?" (v. 60). And so they "drew back and no longer went about with him" (v. 66).

The question the Jews asked on that occasion has troubled much of the world ever since: "How can this man give us his flesh to eat?" (v. 52). How? We theologians have argued the "how" down through the centuries, have responded with more bad arguments than good, have royally excommunicated one another . . . and in the end we fall on our knees and worship humbly in the hymn of St. Thomas Aquinas:

Godhead here in hiding, whom I do adore
Masked by these bare shadows, shape and nothing more:

See, Lord, at thy service low lies here a heart
Lost, all lost in wonder at the God thou art.[2]

Ultimately we take the advice of Jerusalem's bishop to the newly
baptized: Don't judge the reality by what you see and touch and
taste, judge by your "unwavering faith." For as he saw it and put it,
"When the Master himself has explicitly said of the bread, 'This is
my body,' will anyone still dare to doubt? When he is himself our
warranty, saying, 'This is my blood,' who will ever waver and say it
is not his blood?"[3] This is the truth St. Paul "received from the
Lord"; this is the tradition he "delivered" to the Christians of Corinth (1 Cor 11:23); this is the faith we express each time we extend
tongue or hand: "This is the Lamb of God, who takes away the sin
of the world" (Jn 1:29).

We call it the Real Presence. In the Eucharist Jesus is present,
and his presence is real. Not that his presence in our hearts, in the
gathered assembly, in the proclaimed word is not real. Rather because this presence is something special, unique; for it speaks a
unique relation to Jesus' flesh and blood. "My flesh is food indeed,
and my blood is drink indeed" (Jn 6:55).

II

Such is the Eucharistic truth. This is really Jesus' body, really
his blood. My second point: what this basic truth, this Real Presence, does to us. In a word, it gives us life. Unless you eat Jesus'
flesh and drink his blood, "you have no life in you" (Jn 6:53). I do
not mean that your heart stops beating, your brain ceases to function. More importantly, the life of Jesus will not course through
you the way he intended it should.

I am not saying you cannot receive divine life without receiving Holy Communion. Moses and Abraham, Isaiah and Ezekiel
were aflame with God's life; and surely many a noncommunicating
Christian experiences Jesus' promise, "If you love me . . . my Father will love you, and we will come to you and make our home
with you" (Jn 14:23). The heart of the matter is not what is possible because our God is a merciful God who does not want the
death of sinners but that they should live, a God who saves in ever
so many and strange ways. The point is, here is a food which, in its
potential for giving life, is unparalleled.

When you assimilate the food of the body, you change it into your own substance. By a remarkable transformation, a boiled lobster or a greased hamburger becomes you. Quite the opposite happens in the Eucharist. When the Eucharistic Christ gives himself to you as food, you are transformed into him. In the words that Augustine of Hippo heard from on high, "I am the food of grown men and women; grow and you shall eat me. And you shall not change me into yourself, the way bodily food acts; you shall be changed into me." So much so that you can cry out with St. Paul: "It is no longer I who live, but Christ who lives in me" (Gal 2:20). In the felicitous phrase of Pius XII, "If you have received worthily, you are what you have received." In your ceaseless effort to build up Christ in you, the Eucharist is food incomparable; for the food is Christ, body and blood, soul and divinity.

You are what you have received! Is self-pity still possible? Can you continue to moan and groan, to mope and sulk, because your little world passes you by, does not recognize how beautiful you are or how brilliant? What does it matter? You are Christ! Can you even resent the infirmity that eats at your flesh or saps your spirit? After all, if you have been transformed into Christ, you should expect to live the life of the earth-bound Jesus. And that life moves to resurrection only through crucifixion.

III

My third point: What does our Eucharist demand of us? Here a homilist moves in where angels fear to tread. It is one thing to compliment you on being Christ: You are what you have received. It is another thing to question the compliment: Are you really what you have received?

The early Christian writers, the so-called Fathers of the Church, had a remarkable insight. They saw in the Eucharist the consummation, the completion, of the Incarnation. What the physical body of Christ began in Bethlehem, the sacramental body of Christ completes at the altar: the oneness of men and women with God and with one another in the humanity of Christ. Precisely here is the dread demand on us. Our oneness with God in Christ, initiated in the Incarnation, consummated in the Eucharist, must work itself out in a love that is limitless, a love that is all-inclusive, a love that is commanded and justified by the profoundly simple fact that "the other" is always and everywhere Christ.[4] I see demands within your gathering, and demands beyond your assembling.

First, within Catholicism the Bread of Life is not primarily an individualistic thing, a solitary supper, my private party—something between "me and Jesus." Its function is to form a community. St. Paul phrased it beautifully: "Because the bread is one, we, though many, are one body; for we all partake of the one bread" (1 Cor 10:17). The Lord who locks himself in the tabernacle of my body is none other than the Lord who nourishes my next-door neighbor and a far-away pope, the same Christ who feeds the Lebanese, the Japanese, and the Thai, the African, the Cuban, and the Czech. Christ is not divided, Christ is not multiplied. There is one and the same body, one and the same Christ, for all. In his flesh we are one.

But are we? A peril within Catholicism today is that the Eucharist which should make us one often divides us. Catholic communities are unchristianly rent by warring loves. Shall we stand or kneel, pray in an ageless Latin or an ephemeral English, receive Life in our hands or on our tongues, wish peace with a touch or a word, blare forth Bach from an organ or strum a Christian love song? For all too many, these are not academic debates or Christian options; they are life-and-death struggles—so much so that some Catholics call the Vatican II liturgies unorthodox, some will not worship with others save on their own narrow terms, some even suicidally refuse the bread that gives life. Is it for this that the Word-made-flesh offered that flesh the night before he died: "This is my body, which is given for you" (Lk 22:19)?

Which leads to a second issue: the world beyond our altars. A genuinely Eucharistic spirituality means that the Christ of Holy Thursday not only feeds me. He does with me today what he did that night with the bread: He takes me, and he blesses me, and he breaks me . . . and he gives me. Today's feast, Corpus Christi, is not an occasion for narcissism, a chance to fall in love with our own reflection: I am what I have received, I am Christ. It should expand our horizons, force us to focus on the hungers of the human family. In that context—millions of men, women, and children struggling desperately to live human lives, struggling even to live—talk about the Bread of Life can sound awfully empty, suspiciously hollow. And it will be empty, will be hollow, unless we who feed on the Eucharistic Christ are ourselves eucharists for the life of the world.

This is not insubstantial poetry. The Eucharist is central to Christians for a complex of reasons. It is a presence, a real if hidden presence, a presence without peer, a presence of Christ's whole person, a presence which leaps from love and leads to life, a presence which is a promise, a promise of good things which our eyes have not yet seen, our ears not yet heard, blessings it has not entered our minds to imagine. If I am to be a eucharist for the life of the world, my feeding on the flesh of Christ must take me from church to world. I must begin to be present to others, present where they are, present in ways that respond to their needs, to their hungers—for food or freedom, for peace or truth, for understanding or God. I must be really present—I, not merely my money or my mind—somewhat hidden at times but always totally committed, because as a Christian, as Christ, my life is love and only love can bring life, can light dulled eyes with hope, can promise somebody somewhere that tomorrow will be more human, will be worth living.

For you who are what you have received, an urgent question: Where you walk and work, where you play and pray, in the little acre of God you till, is there anyone who is less hungry because you are there?

Dahlgren Chapel
Georgetown University
June 8, 1980

Walter J. Burghardt, S.J.

26
GOD, FREEDOM, CROSS
Feast of St. Ignatius Loyola

- *1 Kings 19:9–15*
- *Galatians 5:16–25*
- *Luke 12:49–53*

Today's three readings are, in part, of my own choosing. The powers that be in liturgy give us fourteen texts from which to select. I have opted for these three because at this moment in my Jesuit existence each leads in a special way to Ignatius and through Ignatius to me. Let me explain.

I

Our first reading, from the First Book of Kings, tells of a cave and of Elijah's experience of God—a God who transpired "not in the wind . . . not in the earthquake . . . not in the fire . . . [but in] a still small voice" (1 Kgs 19:11–12). It brings to mind another cave, the cave at Manresa that set the stage for Ignatius' experience of God.

You remember it, I'm sure. It was late summer 1522. After months of high happiness in purifying fire, after dark nights of the soul enticing to suicide, Ignatius walked out of Manresa to visit an outlying church. On the way, he sat down facing the Cardoner River below. As he sat there, his mind began to open . . . and open . . . and open. It was not a vision; Ignatius insists on that. Rather, he understood realities of earth and heaven with such clarity that everything seemed new to him. He was never able to spell it out. He

163

did indeed confide later to dear colleagues that the illumination had largely to do with God One and Three, with the fashioning of the world and the bodying forth of the Son. But even after three decades it was not so much the what as the how that astonished him, the fresh clarity in his understanding—such clarity that this one experience outstripped all he had learned or been given by God in sixty-two years.

Manresa was for Ignatius what Damascus was for Paul, the burning bush for Moses: a mystery-laden self-revealing of God that initiated his mission, a call to set forth on a shadowed road that would keep opening up as he kept following it.[1] The experience transformed him. Not only on the outside: more presentable and sociable, less harsh and rigid, more human. On a deeper level, it was his inner life that altered. A spirituality that had been individualistic and introspective turned increasingly communitarian and apostolic. And we know that the Cardoner climaxed and crystallized Manresa, gave a new slant to the Spiritual Exercises, and proved a prelude to the formation of the Society of Jesus.

Manresa and the Cardoner tell us something important for Jesuit living. To follow Ignatius, it is not enough to know *about* God; I must know God. In half a century I have learned a great deal *about* God—from philosophy and poetry, from the word of God and the reflection of man. With Aquinas, I have learned that God is Immovable Mover, Uncaused Cause, Necessary Being, Absolute Perfection, Supreme End. With Paul, I have risen from "the things that have been made" to God's "invisible nature," to "His eternal power and deity" (Rom 1:20). I resonate to Joseph Mary Plunkett when he sees Christ's "blood upon the rose,/ And in the stars the glory of his eyes./ His body gleams amid eternal snows,/ His tears fall from the skies." I thrill when I read in Gerard Manley Hopkins that I can find God in man, that "Christ plays in ten thousand places,/ Lovely in limbs, and lovely in eyes not his/ To the Father through the features of men's faces." With John, I believe that the Word of God "became flesh and pitched His tent among us" (Jn 1:14), has made His home within me (Jn 14:23).

But where is my experience of God? Can I say, with Ignatius, that I have "truly encountered God, the living and true God"? That I know "God Himself, not simply human words describing Him"?[2] That this encounter has transformed me, has made me more human, less rigid, more approachable? That it has turned me inside out, made me aware that a direct experience of God, now and at death, is what all our Christian institutions and activities, our Spiritual Exercises and our theology, must have for purpose? With all that I am able to share with others, can I share with them a personal experience of God? The grace of Manresa is not a special privilege granted to Jesuit elite; it is a grace God refuses to no one; it is a grace I must have to live like Ignatius, to be a man seized and possessed by God.

II

This leads felicitously to my second point. The reading from Galatians omits an important Pauline prelude. Just before telling the Galatians to "walk by the Spirit" (5:16), Paul has told them: "You were called to freedom; only do not use your freedom as an opportunity for the flesh, but through love be servants of one another" (5:13). Don't abuse your freedom! How avoid abusing it? Walk by the Spirit! And "if you are led by the Spirit you are not under the law" (5:18).

Ignatius founded a singular type of religious order; for his sons were to harmonize two apparently antithetical virtues: freedom and obedience. You remember how our Rules open. Ignatius would rather not write rules; we should trust Providence and the law of love the Spirit imprints on our hearts; but the Vicar of Christ has appointed otherwise, men will be boys, and so we'll have rules. I've experienced two generations of the Spirit in the Society: early on, when the task of the Spirit was to lead us to the superior, who laid down the law; and later on, when the task of the Spirit was to lead us away from the superior, who had only one vote in a free society.

Not so Ignatius. For him, freedom and obedience had to be kept in fruitful tension; you do not solve the problem by eliminating one or the other. And so he sweated much blood, spilled much ink, reconciling the two; his life and his Exercises bear witness to that. His basic conviction? If the Holy Spirit is really prompting me, He cannot contradict the Spirit prompting the Church. The yardstick of the Spirit is the Church. And if Jesuits today debate whether Ignatius understood "Church" too narrowly here, the fundamental principle must be precious to us all: Our inspiration is the Spirit within the Church.

The principle makes for problems. And our way of playing the principle cannot be taped in advance. In the fifties, I watched sadly as John Courtney Murray returned to the Woodstock Library all his books on religious freedom, on church and state, because he could not write what would be acclaimed as Catholic doctrine a decade later. This year, with pain and pride, I heard our own priest-congressman Robert Drinan say: "As a person of faith I must believe that there is work for me to do which somehow will be more important than the work I am required to leave." On the other hand, many of us must still bear the burden of having to say no to a papal affirmation that has divided the Catholic world.

A chapel is not the place to settle the conflicting claims of freedom and obedience, of Spirit and Church; a certain tension will always be with us. But a chapel *is* the place to suggest that a Jesuit house ought to be a community where all of us who listen to the Spirit can experience love, where all of us are "servants of one another." Servants especially where we differ; understanding even when we cannot agree; where the painful geography of right and left is not allowed to destroy charity—charity that is not cold tolerance but affectionate love. If such is not our house, we must ask ourselves: Are we really walking by the Spirit? How obedient are we? And how free?

III

Experience of God and walking by the Spirit—these introduce a third Jesuit rubric. The "fire" of which Jesus speaks in today's Gospel (Lk 12:49) is not quite the fire of love I intended as a novice to cast upon the earth. It is a figure of judgment, the judgment inseparable from the coming of Jesus and his kingdom. Before that kingdom comes, Jesus must be baptized—submerged by the terrible experience of the cross; the way to the kingdom is through a sea of suffering. And his very coming, his presence, will cause division; men and women have to decide whom they love more: Christ or kin.

Our third rubric is the cross. The centrality of the cross seems symbolized for Ignatius at the Cardoner. When the illumination had lasted for some time, he went to kneel before a wayside cross, to give thanks to his new-found God. A wayside cross. From that moment it would always be the same in the Exercises. Everything would begin and end with Christ's cross; it is the one gateway to glory, the decisive moment of victory over Satan.[3] The radical decision of the Exercises is the decision to remain with Christ crucified. The "more" in Ignatian spirituality is greater and greater conformity with the despised and crucified Christ. Ignatius prays "to be broken with Christ broken." It is summed up wonderfully and fearfully in the phrase he borrowed from Ignatius of Antioch: "My Love has been crucified."[4]

The cross in your life is a sanctuary too intimate for a homilist to invade. But if my own experience is at all typical, I suggest that the Jesuit cross on which we lounge has many a built-in cushion. My Calvary is an occasional cry of the flesh, a hiatal hernia, a burnt-out hamburger; it's the speed of aging and the fear of dying; it's people who question my Catholic loyalty or, worse, bore me. And so I must ask myself: How crucial is the cross of Christ to my everyday living? Can I say honestly with St. Paul: "I rejoice in my sufferings . . . and in my flesh I complete what is lacking in Christ's afflictions for the sake of his body . . . the Church" (Col 1:24)? Not only at the hour of death, but now? Rejoice? Right now my answer would have to be . . . no, not really.

My brothers in Ignatius: The feast of a founder should be a reflection on fidelity. A fearsome task; for fidelity is not slavish reproduction, return to an original Eden, an earlier state of perfection. Fidelity, like reform, calls for a creative response, a living exchange with a new world. How Ignatian is our response, how Jesuit our exchange? I dare not judge. I do know that it will not be Ignatian unless it stems from a personal experience of a living God, openness to the Spirit within the Church, and community with a crucified Christ. On this depends not only our own salvation, but the redemption of those we are privileged to serve.[5]

Dahlgren Chapel
Georgetown University
July 31, 1980

27
BURIED WITH HIM THROUGH BAPTISM
Feast of the Triumph of the Cross

- *Numbers 21:4–9*
- *Philippians 2:6–11*
- *John 3:13–17*

Today a fascinating task confronts you and me. We have to link three realities: the cross we commemorate, the baptism I shall perform, and the community that celebrates both. Cross . . . baptism . . . community. A word on each.

I

Today's feast is a paradox: the Triumph of the Cross. But the paradox is the supreme Christian contradiction: Salvation comes to us through crucifixion—the crucifixion of God-in-flesh. That is the burden of our readings today.

As the years rush on, I am increasingly astounded, shocked, thrilled by the rapturous hymn in Philippians. Though his status was divine, Jesus did not cling like a miser to the glory he had with Yahweh; he emptied himself of it. Instead of seeing in him the glory of the Father, majesty, royalty, dominion, we see in him our own humanity, our weak, tormented, tear-stained flesh. We see someone who looked like the Jew he was; came out of a Jewish girl's body and sucked milk at her breast; learned how to totter and talk, to babble and walk; obeyed a foster father and learned a trade from him; was tempted by the devil and felt the gnawing of hunger; took joy in John and Magdalene, wept over Lazarus and Jerusalem; got tired enough to sleep out a storm in an open boat; whipped trades-

168

men from the Temple and was cast from a cliff by his own towns-people; was betrayed and abandoned by his closest friends; was crowned with thorns and spat upon, stripped naked and nailed to wood; was afraid to die, and died in indescribable agony. No, Jesus did not cling to the glory he had with his Father.

Because he was obedient even unto death, Jesus has become Lord of all creation. Before him every knee must bend; all must proclaim "Jesus Christ is Lord" (Phil 2:11). And because of his obedience unto death we have come to life again: "As Moses lifted up the serpent in the wilderness, so must the Son of Man be lifted up, that whoever believes in him may have eternal life. For God so loved the world that He gave His only Son, that whoever believes in him should not perish but have eternal life. For God sent the Son into the world, not to condemn the world, but that the world might be saved through him" (Jn 3:14–17). Through his death we are free: free from the law, from sin, from death, from ourselves. He who was slave is Lord; we who were slaves are free. Here indeed is the triumph of the cross.

II

The triumph of Christ's cross leads to my second point: How link this cross to baptism? In a few short moments I shall pour baptismal water over a Georgetown student. Karen has already experienced the faith of which St. Paul speaks so often and so eloquently.[1] She has heard the word about Christ—largely in the Dahlgren community—and in consequence she has committed her whole person to Christ. With her lips she acknowledges that "Jesus is Lord," and with her mind she believes that "God raised him from the dead" (Rom 10:9). Not just an intellectual assent to propositions; more importantly, a personal commitment that engages her whole self to Christ in all her relations with God, with the images of God, with God's world. And so she can repeat with Paul: "Now even the physical life I am living I live through faith in the Son of God, who loved me and gave himself for me" (Gal 2:20). Her faith is obedience to God's call in Christ.

It is not Karen's own doing. The faith of a Christian is a gift from above: "It is by [Christ's] favor that you have been saved through faith; and this does not come from you, it is the gift of God" (Eph 2:8). The initiative rests with God; He has spoken, has called, has invited; and Karen, in full freedom, has answered yes. And this free response, spoken in the full flush of her young adulthood, is a call to service: "In union with Christ Jesus" the only thing that matters is "faith acting through love" (Gal 5:6). "Through love be servants of one another" (v. 13).

But for Paul, as for us, faith is tied to baptism. Here is where the believer puts on Christ, is "consecrated and made upright" (1 Cor 6:11). But even more important in the context of today's feast, Paul insists that what baptism does is to identify the new Christian with the dying-rising Christ. "Through baptism we have been buried with him in death, so that just as he was raised from the dead through the Father's glory, we too may live a new life. For if we have grown into union with him by undergoing a death like his, of course we shall do so by being raised to life like him" (Rom 6:4–5).

Baptism images the dying and rising of Christ. This mystical, sacramental dying with Christ in order to rise with him was more vividly symbolized in the Church's earlier days than it is now. Then you might have descended into a genuine pool. And you would have experienced what a fourth-century bishop explained to his freshly baptized in Jerusalem:

> . . . you were conducted to the sacred pool of divine baptism, as Christ passed from the cross to the sepulchre you see before you. You were asked, one by one, whether you believed in the name of the Father and of the Son and of the Holy Spirit; you made that saving confession, and then you dipped thrice under the water and thrice rose up again, therein mystically signifying Christ's three days' burial. . . . In the same moment you were dying and being born, and that saving water was at once your grave and your mother. . . .
>
> The strange, the extraordinary, thing is that we did not really die, nor were really buried or really crucified; nor did we really rise again. This was figurative and symbolic; yet our salvation was real. Christ's crucifixion was real, his burial was real, and his resurrection was real; and all these he has freely made ours, that by sharing his sufferings in a symbolic enactment we may really and truly gain salvation. Oh, too generous love! Christ received the nails in his immaculate hands and feet; Christ felt the pain; and on me without pain or labor, through the fellowship of his pain, he freely bestows salvation.[2]

No, baptism is not a physical dying, not a matter of nails and wood, of God's abandonment and man's mockery, of a last agonizing gasp. And still Karen dies—to all that has kept her enslaved; and she rises "a new creation" (2 Cor 5:17; Gal 6:15), alive with the risen life of Christ. She is incorporated into Christ: From this time forth, *through* Christ she is *with* Christ and *in* Christ. She can cry with St. Paul: "I have been crucified with Christ; it is no longer I who live, but Christ who lives in me; and the life I now live in the flesh I live by faith in the Son of God, who loved me and gave himself for me" (Gal 2:20). Here indeed is the triumph of the cross.

III

But for Karen to be baptized into the dying-rising Christ is not a drama with one actress; it is not something you and I watch, like spectators in a theatre. If baptism incorporates Karen into Christ, it incorporates her into the whole Christ, into the body of Christ. Today she enters a fresh, unique union with all Christians, with us. Recall the words of Paul: "We have all been baptized . . . to form one body" (1 Cor 12:13). Like each of us, Karen reaches salvation by identifying with a community of salvation, a saving community. That is why Paul compares baptism to Israel's passage through the Reed Sea (1 Cor 10:1–2). In the waters of baptism the new Israel is fashioned, a new people.

Karen's baptism, therefore, is not a superfluous ceremony, nice icing on the cake of her faith. It does something real: It plunges her sacramentally into Christ, and in doing so it makes her part of Christ's Church. Not magic, but the power of Christ touched to words and water.

This places on each of us, on the Christian community, a fearful responsibility. Not a guilt trip; a responsibility. We no longer belong to ourselves; we belong to Christ and to one another. "If one member suffers," Paul proclaims, "all suffer together; if one member is honored, all rejoice together" (1 Cor 13:26). Karen's pilgrimage to God is now linked to the community—in a special way, to this community. In some measure, perhaps in large measure, she will move towards God or away from Him depending on what the rest of the body does, how we live and love, how we play and pray, how we suffer and joy.

And so, in Karen's baptism we must renew our own. We too reject sin, the glamor of evil, Satan. We too profess our belief in God the Father, in Christ who was crucified and rose again, in the

Holy Spirit, in God's forgiveness and our resurrection, in life everlasting. And when I confirm her, we will pray God to send His Spirit on *us*, to give *all* of us "the spirit of wisdom and understanding, the spirit of right judgment and courage, the spirit of knowledge and reverence, the spirit of wonder and awe in [God's] presence."

Here indeed is the triumph of the cross—that all of us who have been baptized into Christ relive his dying and his rising, his dying to himself and living to God, his total gift of himself for the sin-scarred children of Adam. Here, in this chapel and outside, here is the triumph of the cross—in Karen and in you.

Dahlgren Chapel
Georgetown University
September 14, 1980

28
THIS IS THE TEMPLE OF THE LORD
Feast of the Dedication of St. John Lateran (C)

- *1 Kings 8:22–23, 27–30*
- *Ephesians 2:19–22*
- *Matthew 5:23–24*

At first sight, today's feast may well baffle the homilist. Dedication of a Roman basilica? Here at Georgetown, U.S.A.? Oh yes, St. John Lateran is "mother and chief of all the churches of [Rome] and the world." It was built by Emperor Constantine on ground belonging to the Laterani family. It has a fascinating history and striking architecture. It, and not St. Peter's, is the pope's cathedral. But after you've said that much, what more is left to say? What remains for the human spirit questing for God? Surprisingly, a great deal. Our three readings combine to suggest some profoundly religious reflections. Three readings, three points.

I

First, the reading from Kings (1 Kgs 8:22–23, 27–30). It is Solomon's prayer at the dedication of the temple in Jerusalem. He knows we cannot imprison God in a place: "Behold, heaven and the highest heaven cannot contain thee; how much less this house which I have built!" (v. 27). And still he can say: "This house [is] the place of which thou hast said, 'My name shall be there'" (v. 29). That is to say, God Himself will be there. His name is His presence; the name of God stands for God Himself.

But is not God everywhere? He is indeed; He is present to every nook and cranny of His universe. He *has* to be; otherwise He would not be God. He *is* everywhere because He is *active* every-where, because without Him the sun could not shine nor the snow-flake fall; without Him the grass could not grow nor the seas surge; without Him the skylark could not sing, the panther prowl, the shad ascend the rivers. If He were not wherever I am, I would sim-ply not *be.*

Then why single out special spots? Not for God's sake; for our own. We need places that are specially sacred because here we feel sure God comes to meet His people. It need not have a roof. It can be the top of Mount Sinai, where the Lord appeared to Moses veiled in fire (Exod 3:2; 19:20). And remember how Jacob heard God in a dream: "The land on which you lie I will give to you and your descendants" (Gen 28:13)? Awaking, he said, "Surely the Lord is in this place. . . . How awesome is this place! This is none other than the house of God, and this is the gate of heaven" (vv. 16–17). Remember the portable sanctuary by which God could re-side permanently among the people He led across the desert? The tabernacle, the tent, was the place where the people encountered their God, where God dwelt among the cherubim, gave His ora-cles, at once hid and revealed Himself.

In all religions there are sacred places—places where men and women are sure that divinity makes itself present to them, to re-ceive their worship and to make them share in divine favor and di-vine life.[1]

II

Second, the reading from Ephesians (Eph 2:19–22). Negative-ly, it can remind us of Jeremiah's warning to Israel: "Do not trust in these deceptive words: 'This is the temple of the Lord, the tem-ple of the Lord, the temple of the Lord' " (Jer 7:4). A sacred place can become a superstition. Solomon's temple, the Lateran basilica, Dahlgren Chapel—these sacred sites do not suffice for salvation. As the Lord said through the mouth of Isaiah:

> What is the house which you would build for me,
>   and what is the place of my rest? . . .
> But this is the man to whom I will look,
>   he that is humble and contrite in spirit,
>   and trembles at my word.
>
> (Isa 66:1–2)

Positively, Ephesians sums up a fresh theology of temple. For all his reverence for the old temple—it is the house of God, a house of prayer, the house of his Father—Jesus announced a new temple. Remember his mystery-laden words in Jerusalem: "Destroy this temple, and in three days I will raise it up"? John tells us what he meant: "He was speaking of the temple of his body" (Jn 2:19, 21). The new sign of God's presence among us is the body of Jesus. Here, above all, is where the God whom heaven cannot contain has chosen to dwell; here the Word of God has "pitched His tent" (Jn 1:14). To this presence of God there is no parallel; here divinity dwells as nowhere else: God and human flesh are one person!

But there is more to the miracle of God's new dwelling on earth. The physical temple that is the body of Jesus is prolonged in the spiritual temple that is his Church. Through Christ "the whole structure is fitted together and takes shape as a holy temple in the Lord" (Eph 2:21). Here is a new body of Christ, a body that is so intimately linked to Christ that St. Paul calls him "the head of the body" (Col 1:18). Oh yes, we have our temples of stone and wood, where God comes to encounter His people. But the more important temple is the living temple, the people itself. "You form a building which rises on the foundation of the apostles and prophets, with Christ Jesus himself as the cornerstone" (Eph 2:20). The most important truth about this building is not its hierarchical structure, a pyramid that has pope at the apex, all manner of clergy down the sides, laity at the base. What makes the Church of Christ a temple is that God dwells therein, the Holy Spirit gives it life and love from within; it is a privileged sign of God's presence in the world, a privileged place of encounter between divinity and humanity. Little wonder the First Epistle of Peter proclaims: "Like living stones, be yourselves built into a spiritual house, to be a holy priesthood, to offer spiritual sacrifices acceptable to God through Jesus Christ. . . . You are a chosen race, a royal priesthood, a holy nation, God's own people, that you may declare the wonderful deeds of Him who called you out of darkness into His marvelous light" (1 Pet 2:5, 9).

More marvelous still, each of you "is being built into [this temple], to become a dwelling place of God in the Spirit" (Eph 2:22). Each of you is a shrine, a sacred place. For if you love him, Christ assured you, if you keep his word, Father and Son come to you and make their home with you (Jn 14:23). You are a tabernacle where the Trinity is tented. That is why Paul was so harsh with sexual license. "Do you not know that your body [your living body, your real self] is a temple of the Holy Spirit within you?" (1 Cor 6:19). *You* are a temple of God. Temples of stone make no sense without temples of flesh. Dahlgren is a mockery if here you meet only your friends and not God, if the God who is present here is not present within you.

III

Third, the reading from Matthew (Mt 5:23–24). The passage is brief: "If you are offering your gift at the altar, and there remember that your brother [or sister] has something against you, leave your gift there before the altar and go, first be reconciled to your brother [or sister], and then come and offer your gift." That command is understandable. If you, temple of the Spirit, are responsible for disunity, if you have destroyed love, then you are not ready to greet God in the temple where He comes to meet His people. You have to cleanse your own temple first.

That Gospel reading warns us, more subtly indeed than did Jeremiah, against superstitious reliance on a temple of stone: "This is the temple of the Lord, the temple of the Lord, the temple of the Lord." If you want to desecrate Dahlgren, come here convinced that this temple can save you. We are a saved community, we go to Dahlgren 12:15!

Oh yes, God's mighty deeds are remembered here, re-presented here. God encounters us here. He comes to meet us in our very gathering together; He is present in His word proclaimed; He becomes sacramentally present when I murmur "This is my body"; we feed on the flesh of Christ and taste his blood; we find the face of Christ on the faces about us. This is indeed a remarkable place, a sacred place; for we are sure that God is here.

And still the temple of stone does not save. The pregnant question is, what sort of temple does this temple make of *us?* Can we say sincerely with St. Paul that our "whole structure . . . is taking shape as a holy temple in the Lord," that in Christ "you are being built into this temple, to become a dwelling place for God in the Spirit" (Eph 2:21–22)? This body of Christ that is the people of God, this Church in miniature that is our community, is it what it was created to be, a sign to the nations that God has come, that God is here? Is not the Church's internal warfare a scandal to outsiders, provocation to the skeptical to crow: "Look how these Christians hate one another"? It is not unbelievers who are bloodying the soft face of Ireland. It is not Jews or Moslems who are killing forty to fifty people a day in El Salvador. It is not just infidels who pollute earth and sky, the rivers and the sea; not just infidels who, in Paul's words, "take the members of Christ and make them members of a prostitute" (1 Cor 6:15); not just infidels who are terrorists, slum landlords, Mafiosi. It is not only non-Christians who stand by and do . . . nothing.

Today's Gospel suggests that we who come together here are in many ways divided. Divided from one another, divided from those outside these doors. We come here to be healed. No, the temple of stone does not heal; but here we can be healed. The first step is a giant step. The first step is to come here and acknowledge our separateness, ask forgiveness for our divisions, promise to repair the rifts. The first step is simply to encounter God and one another in our naked, sinful humanness.

In this context the Gospel reading is not just one example of division; it sums up the heart of our Christian existence. We cannot build up the temple of God that is the Church, the shrine of the Spirit that is our own self, in some splendid isolation, in a desert of our private designing. If no Christian is an island, no Christian is a solitary temple. At least not if you want your temple of flesh to come alive, to glow and grow. And you come alive, you become a living temple, to the extent that you are related in love. *This* is the temple of the Lord.

Do you want to discover how actually alive you are in the Spirit? Simply ask yourself: Whom do I really love?

Dahlgren Chapel
Georgetown University
November 9, 1980

your reach others

oh say YES!

Be witnesses

Letting it BE

It happened to ME!

MEDLEY

29
YOU ARE WITNESSES
Evangelization Day for Bishops,
Priests, and Deacons

- *Isaiah 52:7–10*
- *Ephesians 3:2–12*
- *Luke 24:46–53*

At the risk of resisting Rome and tradition, I shall not preach "evangelization." The word is too big for a homily; it is dreadfully abstract; it has lost the flavor of the Greek "good news"; it suggests the worst of Christian TV hard-sell. The idea itself is captured more captivatingly in today's Gospel: "You are witnesses of these things" (Lk 24:48), and in today's theme: "You are my witnesses." You . . . are . . . witnesses. These three words are the key to your gathering, the key to your ministry, the key to your lives. The three words are my three points.

I

First, you are *witnesses.* Now what does it mean to be a witness? In its fullest meaning, I am a witness not simply if I see something, not simply if I affirm that something is true. I am a first-rate witness if I do both: if I testify to something I have myself experienced. I have seen Lady Diana wed Prince Charles; I have heard Beethoven's *Fifth*; I have tasted Veal Saltimbocca; I have smelled the aroma of Brut; I have kissed the Blarney stone. And I tell you about the experience.

The First Letter of John is a thrilling example of what I mean: "That which was from the beginning, which we have heard, which we have seen with our eyes, which we have looked upon and

181

touched with our hands, concerning the word of life—the life was
made manifest, and we saw it, and testify to it, and proclaim to you
the eternal life which was with the Father and was made manifest to
us—that which we have seen and heard we proclaim also to you" (1
Jn 1:1–3).

As witnesses to Jesus, the apostles were without peer. They
walked with him, talked with him, fished with him, ate with him,
prayed with him. Peter clutched his hand when he began to sink;
Thomas put his fingers into his side. They saw him after he rose
from the dead, watched as he was lifted from their sight on a
mountain in Galilee. Little wonder that they could testify to him,
witness to him "in Judea and Samaria and to the end of the earth"
(Acts 1:8). Little wonder that Peter could preach: "This Jesus God
raised up, and of that we are all witnesses" (Acts 2:32). Little wonder that untold men and women "were cut to the heart," asked the
apostles: "Brethren, what shall we do?" (Acts 2:37). Little wonder
that thousands upon thousands repented of their sins, were baptized, received the gift of the Spirit. Little wonder that "the company of those who believed were of one heart and soul" (Acts 4:32).

For the apostles had seen, had heard, had touched. Theirs was
no academic Christology, no scholastic soteriology. They had been
grasped by a Person. They had been called in person—from the
lake and the countinghouse. They had died with him and risen with
him. They were loved by him and they loved him.

II

Second, *you* are witnesses. Like the apostles, you too testify to
Jesus. You declare that at the midpoint of history God took flesh of
a virgin; that this God-man proclaimed a kingdom not of this
world, preached forgiveness of sins and a new birth of freedom;
that for us and for our salvation he died a criminal's death, rose
from the rock, lifted our humanity to his Father; that he is Lord of
the living and the dead; that this risen Lord lives in us through the
Spirit he has given to us; that in this Christian community we find
our forgiveness, his flesh, God's love; that if we share his passion
we will experience his resurrection, live with him days without end.

To all this you testify, and rightly so. But simply to testify is
not enough. What the world outside these walls asks of you is that
you attest what you have seen, proclaim what you have heard, tes-

tify to what you have touched. What today's men and women look for in you, expect from you, is some sign that you have experienced what you are proclaiming. I am not questioning the objective validity of the sacraments. However sluggish or sleepy you are, as long as you mumble the right words and pour water and not beer, the devil flees and we have another Catholic. God does not (thank God) leave redemption entirely in our hands. I am saying that you will "evangelize" effectively only if you yourself are a sort of sacrament, a symbol, an outward sign of inward grace. You will move hearts only if it comes through to them that you have seen Jesus, have been fired by his presence, have experienced that presence in yourself and in the assembly, in the preached word and in the blessed bread.

Put another way, you will touch hearts if you know God. Not simply know *about* God. You and I know a good deal about God. Less than we think, but more than most. We have argued to God from sheer reason; we believe realities God has revealed; we are graced with what Vatican I called "a remarkably fruitful understanding of mysteries."

But that is not enough—not by half. You must know God. I am not speaking of something extraordinary: Moses addressed from a burning bush, Augustine's vision at Ostia, Joan of Arc's "voices," Catherine of Siena's mystical espousals, Ignatius Loyola inexpressibly illumined about God One and Three. Such experiences do happen; they can happen to you. More commonly, our experience is less startling. We grow gradually into intimacy with a Person; we are increasingly absorbed by a presence. A *living* presence more real than the room around us, as real as the priest next to you. A *holy* presence that fills us with awe and fear, the while it warms and draws us. An unspeakable *loneliness,* for in the presence of Love we are fearfully far from Love. Within sorrow a profound *joy* that will not be imprisoned, must break forth to be shared with others.[1]

As in Gospel days, so now, there is one thing the Gentiles want before all else—what they asked of Philip: "Sir, we would like to see Jesus" (Jn 12:21). They will see him more easily if *you* have seen him.

III

This leads naturally to my third point: You *are* witnesses. It is the difference between doing and being—better still, the wedding of the two. You will indeed have to do something; I am not down-grading programs of evangelization, techniques, tapes and TV, practical skills. But far more important is who you *are*. Mother Teresa is doing remarkable things for the skin-and-bones starving in Calcutta. Still more remarkable is who she is, how she comes through to people. That once cantankerous journalist Malcolm Muggeridge tells movingly how he put Mother Teresa on a train in Calcutta: "When the train began to move, and I walked away, I felt as though I were leaving behind me all the beauty and all the joy in the universe. Something of God's love has rubbed off on Mother Teresa."[2] I suspect it stems from her own intense realization of what Christian action, Christian doing, is all about. When asked if she does not get discouraged in her work with the destitute and the dying, she replied: "God has not called me to be successful. He has called me to be faithful."

Let me make an uncommonly honest confession. In forty years as a priest, I have changed enormously. I still treasure the objective truth neo-scholastic philosophy impressed on me; I still venerate the word of God in Scripture and the word of man from Rome. But for two decades I have experienced a Catholic revolution. The clear and distinct idea is not enough, and the word is rarely imper-sonal, disembodied, a dictionary entry. Uncounted Catholics are as moved by *my* faith as by *the* faith—sometimes more. It is not enough for them that I speak with the clarity of Descartes, with the objectivity of Einstein, with the authority of the Church. They are looking behind the words to a person, behind what I say to who I am.

It is splendidly symbolized, expressively exemplified, in our li-turgical changes. When I face God's people as I now must, the stress is no longer exclusively on the eternal Priest, on the hidden Christ; *I* now transpire, come to light. No longer do all close their eyes and pillow the Host on their tongues; most take the Christ in their hands and look into my eyes. What they see there lifts them up or depresses them, warms their faith or chills it. They judge from my face, from my fingers, from my flesh whether I joy in the Eucharist, in Christ, in the Church, in human living, in them. If *I* care, they feel that Christ cares. If *I* weep, they sense that Christ is crying.

It is a fearful responsibility, this fresh expectation people have of you. At the same time it is a thrilling challenge to your priesting, to your "deaconing," to your witnessing. It can deliver you from that damnable temptation to judge your ministry by functions, to divide your life into the sacred and the secular. In your life there is nothing secular save sin. By a special sacrament your public office is to bear witness to Jesus. Not only at the altar, not only in "the box" or the pulpit, but every moment. You *are* a priest; you *are* a deacon.

That is why you have to be a man of prayer, aware of God's presence—at times, of His absence. A man of the cross, making up in your own flesh what is wanting to the sufferings of Jesus. A man whose celibacy does not make you prematurely senile, the proverbial crotchety bachelor, but releases you for warm human relations that draw people not only to you but to Christ. A man who, like St. Paul, "will most gladly spend and be spent" for others (2 Cor 12:15). A man who joys in playing priest or deacon, would not exchange it for any other calling in the world.

If such you are, then your approach to evangelizing can be the approach of the apostles: not proof but witness. You testify to what you have seen and heard and touched. In so testifying, you can be as priestly from a wheelchair as from a sanctuary or a soup kitchen. For "God has not called [you] to be successful. He has called [you] to be faithful." He has called you to . . . be.[3]

Civic Center
Hartford, Connecticut
August 21, 1981

30
SHOULD ANYONE SAY FOREVER?
Wedding Homily 1

- *1 Corinthians 2:9–12*
- *Philippians 3:9–14*
- *John 6:44–51*

Several years ago a dear Jesuit friend authored a small book with a challenging title: *Should Anyone Say Forever?*[1] Should anyone say "forever"? For us here, that question has a past, a present, and a future. A word about each.

I

Should anyone say "forever"? The question has a past; it leaps out of your experience and mine. In a short lifetime I have seen my world move from a way of thinking where "forever" was a household word to a way of living where "forever" seems unreal. Nothing lasts forever. Whether it's peace or justice, friendship or faith, money or fame, a suntan or a car, life or love—nothing lasts forever. All sorts of people—priests and politicians, men and women, believers and atheists—have vowed fidelity forever: to a person or a place, to an institution or to God. But times change; ideals die; good Christians convert; neighborhoods go down; governments topple. New offers are too attractive to pass up—for models or quarterbacks, for coaches or executives.

And, high on the list of perishables, marriage does not last. The casualty list, fifty percent, is a tragic suggestion that "forever" is not a thunderous promise but a tremulous hope. Is it realistic for me to say to any couple, in the lovely words of an older exhortation at marriage, "And so, not knowing what lies before you, you take each other for better or worse, for richer or poorer, in sickness and in health, until death do you part"?

II

Our question, then, must move into the present, into today's celebration. Should *this* couple, should Margaret and David, say "forever"? My response is a resounding yes. For two reasons. First, because the yes they will murmur to each other stems not simply from themselves, from their own free choice. The profound stimulus for their "forever" is proclaimed in today's reading from First Corinthians: "The Spirit [they] have received is not the world's spirit but the Spirit that is from God, helping [them] to recognize the gifts God has given [them]" (1 Cor 2:12). The gift, the power, is from God. He it is who brought them together; He it is who inspired their love; He it is who makes it possible for them to say "forever." And so their promise is not a prediction; it is not a marital barometer, a forecast of fair weather. It is their way of saying to each other: "By God's grace, I give you my all; I give you all I am, all I hope to be. By God's grace. . . ."

This points up the second reason why David and Margaret can say "forever." They bring to each other a unique gift. You see, among many marvels of this marvelous day is that this ceremony is a sacrament. A singular sacrament. Of this sacrament alone the priest is not the minister; he does not make them man and wife. The ministers of this sacrament are David and Margaret. And this means that they are channels of grace to each other. David and Margaret, when you murmur yes, you will give to each other two priceless gifts. You will give to each other . . . yourselves; and you will give to each other . . . God. With Him to share your future, you can dare to say "forever."

III

Your future. Yes, our question has a future. Today is only the beginning of forever. For all its uncertainty, it promises to be a glorious adventure. I say this especially in the light of a remarkable axiom of philosophical and Christian wisdom. In the language of philosophers, the choices I make determine who I am. In the language of saints, we become what we love. History tells me that if I set my heart on power, I may come out a Hitler. Theology tells me that if I love God I am divinized, I share in God's own being, I become like God.

And so it will be with Margaret and David. In loving, you will not only be giving. In loving, you will be given, you will be shaped. Oh yes, you will remain free, will be each your own person. But that person will be subtly, ceaselessly fashioned by the other. Not manipulation, but love—love that paradoxically should bind you together and free you to be yourselves. And since love's shaping is an endless task, never perfect here below, for that reason too it is a good thing that you say "forever."

It will not be easy, especially in surroundings where few men and women dare to say "forever." You will bleed and you will weep. For that I have no panacea, no instant cure. I can only remind you of a remarkable conviction which the late French author François Mauriac recorded, to be released after his death: "I believe, as I did as a child, that life has meaning, a direction, a value; that no suffering is lost, that every tear counts, each drop of blood, that the secret of the world is to be found in St. John's . . . 'God is Love.' "[2]

No suffering need be lost; every tear can count. But to ensure that it does, you need not only God's love, not only your own. You need a community of love. You need the dear people who surround you today, who celebrate your love in this lovely chapel. "No man," said Thomas Merton, "enters heaven all by himself." Similarly, no man and woman can live their "forever" all by themselves. And so, on this promising, perilous day, we promise you not only our prayers, not only sterling silver or fondue forks. We promise you a support which your daring "forever" inspires in us. This day we renew our own commitments and covenants, shopworn perhaps, tarnished by time, dulled by routine, dented by experience, scraped by cynicism and skepticism. This day, thanks to you, we say a fresh yes: to God, to our tear-stained world, to one another, and in a special way to you. . . . Forever.

Dahlgren Chapel
Georgetown University
August 30, 1980

31
FOR EVERYTHING WHICH IS YES
Wedding Homily 2

- *1 Corinthians 13:4–13*
- *Matthew 6:25–33*

Susanne and Stefan: A wedding is not a time for much preaching. For all its public nature, the event we celebrate is inviolably private. Not mine, then, to discourse on love. Not mine to tell you what your love means to *you*. Only a word witnessing what your love means to *us*.

I would call today's celebration a resounding yes. On three levels. First, it is a yes to *life*. Your yes to each other is a striking affirmation that life is not genuinely lived unless it is shared. A paradox indeed. The more you give of life, the more alive you are. You will discover this as you grow in love, as you mature and ripen, expand and deepen. You will discover it if your love bears fruit in living images of that love, living likenesses of your flesh and spirit. And so you let go—let go of so much that is past, so much that was the private, individual you. From now on, to have life you must share life. You are no longer your own; you are of each other, for each other.

Second, your yes is a yes to *love*. The passage you have plucked from Paul is a favorite of brides and grooms. Understandably so, for it is a peerless paean to love. "If I have not love, I am nothing" 1 (Cor 13:2). Love towers above faith and hope (v. 13). "Love bears all things, believes all things, hopes all things. . . . Love never ends" (vv. 7–8). What you realize, and many do not, is the kind of love Paul is talking about. It is, as Paul told the Christians of Rome, "God's love . . . poured into [your] hearts through the Holy Spirit who has been given to [you]" (Rom 5:5). It is love in Christ. Such is

189

the love that "is patient and kind, not jealous or boastful, not arrogant or rude, does not strive for its own advantage, is neither irritable nor resentful, does not rejoice at wrong, rejoices in the truth" (1 Cor 13:4–6). Such is the love that "never ends" (v. 8). Your love is a sharing in God's love.

Third, your yes is a yes to *God.* You have chosen an intriguing Gospel reading, unusual for a wedding. "Do not be anxious . . ." (Mt 7:25). Not be anxious? Today? When blood reddens Iran and Iraq? When atomic annihilation threatens the earth? When a fourth of the world is hungry? When you and I perch on the edge of a depression? In this context, only your commitment to a loving God could call forth from you this marriage maxim: "Seek first the kingdom of God." It suggests that you may indeed be anxious, justifiably anxious, but that you are resting your love tranquilly and trustfully in God. "Your heavenly Father knows that you need all these things" (Mt 6:32). What He will do about "all these things," you know not. You know only that God is your Father. And so you murmur with confidence: "Father, into thy hands . . ." (Lk 23:46).

A resounding yes to life, to love, to God. I can think of nothing more appropriate with which to introduce the marriage ceremony than the joyous eucharist of the poet e. e. cummings:

> i thank You God for most this amazing
> day: for the leaping greenly spirits of trees
> and a blue true dream of sky: and for everything
> which is natural which is infinite which is yes
>
> (i who have died am alive again today,
> and this is the sun's birthday; this is the birth
> day of life and of love and wings: and of the gay
> great happening illimitably earth)
>
> how should tasting touching hearing seeing
> breathing any—lifted from the no
> of all nothing—human merely being
> doubt unimaginable You?
>
> (now the ears of my ears awake and
> now the eyes of my eyes are opened)[1]

Yes, we thank you, God, for most this amazing day: for every-

thing which is natural, for everything which is infinite, for everything which is yes.

Dahlgren Chapel
Georgetown University
October 11, 1980

32
LORD, IF YOU HAD BEEN HERE
Homily for a Mass of the Resurrection

• *John 11:20–27*

When Adele asked me whether I had a special Gospel reading for this morning, I was brash enough to say yes. It is a segment from the Lazarus story. The background is woven of emotion and mystery. Lazarus has fallen ill. Since Jesus has been awfully close to him, his sisters, Mary and Martha, send word to Jesus—a touching message: "Lord, he whom you love is ill" (Jn 11:3). The Evangelist John then puts together two puzzling sentences: "Now Jesus loved Martha and her sister and Lazarus. So when he heard that [Lazarus] was ill, he stayed two days longer in the place where he was" (Jn 11:5–6). When he finally reaches Bethany, Lazarus is dead four days. Then comes our Gospel passage:

> When Martha heard that Jesus was coming, she went and met him, while Mary sat in the house. Martha said to Jesus: "Lord, if you had been here, my brother would not have died. And even now I know that whatever you ask from God, God will give you." Jesus said to her: "Your brother will rise again." Martha said to him: "I know that he will rise again in the resurrection at the last day." Jesus said to her: "I am the resurrection and the life. He who believes in me, though he die, yet shall he live, and whoever lives and believes in me shall never die. Do you believe this?" She said to him: "Yes, Lord; I believe that you are the Christ, the Son of God, he who is coming into the world."

That inspired passage speaks to me in two ways, on two levels. It reproduces the emotion in our hearts and it repeats the mystery-laden message of Jesus. A word on each.

192

I

First, the Gospel passage re-creates our very human reactions. Often in the past forty-eight hours I have felt like saying with Martha, "Lord, if you had [really] been here, our brother would not have died." Where were you when we needed you? "Lord," we said so often, "he whom you love is ill." And nothing happened. Wherever you were, you just stayed there—stayed there until he whom you love was dead.

The reaction is understandable. Here is a young man, half my age; the richest part of his life has only begun. He is highly intelligent, good in the strong sense of the word, shaped in equal parts of humor and love. His wedding day, I'm convinced, was planned in heaven. In a world bent by anger and hate, by ambition and suspicion, he is remarkably open and friendly, generous and trusting, a wonderful welding of karate and gentleness. And he loves—loves God and people, loves wife and life—dear God, how passionately in love he is with life!

And without warning life is stolen from him. Not swiftly and painlessly; no, slowly and cruelly. So once again, as with my brother wasting away at 27, as with a score of black Atlanta lads brutally murdered, I cannot help asking: Lord, where were you? When he whom you loved was dying, where were you?

There is no answer that will satisfy the philosopher. Like Job in the Old Testament, we do not understand. In the face of evil, of innocent suffering, human wisdom is bankrupt. And as for Job, so for us, peace will come only from trust, from a resounding cry of faith that, despite all the evidence, God still cares, God still loves—loves Joe, loves Adele, loves us. "God so loved the world that He gave His only Son" (Jn 3:16).

But remember, trust stems not from proof but from love. When God finally showed His face to an anguished Job, a rebellious Job, God said nothing to him about his guilt or innocence, nothing about suffering and its meaning. God did not explain. And Job did not say: "Ah yes, now I understand. Thank you." No, to encounter God is to experience not explanation but love. Love God as you love Joe, with the same intensity, unreservedly, and you will "see" in the darkness that God has richer plans for us than we have for ourselves.

Where were you, Lord, these last few months? Closer to Joe

than ever before. For every Gethsemane is your garden, and every Calvary is your cross. Thank you for being with Joe as he shared your agony; thank you for being near him as he died your death.

II

Secondly, the Gospel passage repeats the mystery-laden message of Jesus. What is that message? Very simply . . . life.

As you listened to the Gospel, did you notice that Jesus was not satisfied with Martha's act of faith? Oh yes, she believed, believed in life—but in *another* life: "I know that [my brother] will rise again in the resurrection at the last day" (Jn 11:24). No, says Jesus, that's not the point. "Whoever lives and believes in me shall never die" (Jn 11:26). Shall *never* die.

This is not pious exaggeration. This is not spiritual pap, soft food for feeble Christians, a sop for those who mourn. For me, the most rapturous, the most consoling words in the Gospel are the short words our Lord spoke to his apostles the night before he died: "I live, and you will live" (Jn 14:19). More exactly, "I have life, and [so] you will have life." Here is the pith, the marrow, of John's Gospel, summed up in today's reading: "Jesus said to [Martha]: 'I am . . . the life' " (Jn 11:25). Jesus not only *has* life, he *is* life—because the Holy Spirit, that Spirit who gives life, is his Spirit; and this Spirit, this life, this Spirit of life, he gives to us. In John's vision, in the Christian vision, a man dies only if and when the Spirit of life leaves him. At the moment Jesus "bowed his head and gave up his Spirit" (Jn 19:30), he was gloriously alive, because the Spirit of life, the Holy Spirit, was still and forever his Spirit, his life.

And so for Joe. Indeed, there is much to mourn, as there was much to mourn on Calvary. We shall have to wait for "the resurrection at the last day" (Jn 11:24) before we see the smile light up his eyes again, before we feel the gentle pressure of his touch. And that is sad, no matter how profound our faith. But the thrilling truth remains: Joe is alive! Alive with the life of Christ, because even in death the Holy Spirit never left him. More alive than he ever was before, because every tear is past, every malignant growth, every infirmity of our fragile humanity. In the presence of God, there is only God, there is only love.

And we who remain, what of us? We have our memories, of course, and they are precious. Like Mary in Bethlehem—and after

Calvary—we can "[keep] all these things, pondering them in [our] heart" (Lk 2:19). But there is more, much more. Joe is not merely a memory; he is part of us, part and parcel of each one of us. He is inescapably built into our lives. How? I cannot speak for you, only for myself. Who and what I am, Joe has helped immeasurably to shape. His courage and his laughter, his Christian confidence and his limitless love, these have seeped into my blood. Because of Joe, I am more priestly, more Christian, more human. Can any of you say less?

Adele, dear parents, warm friends: For the way he lived, Joe is alive with God. By the way we live, let us keep him alive in ourselves.

Cathedral of the Holy Cross
Boston, Massachusetts
March 14, 1981

33
BLESSED ARE THE PEACEMAKERS
Memorial Mass for Mohamed el Sadat

- *Lamentations 3:17–26*
- *Matthew 5:1–9*

"Blessed are the peacemakers,
for they shall be called children of God."
(Mt 5:9)

I

Lord, we come before you wonderfully and fearfully different. Some of us have our best years behind us; the lives of others lie ahead. Some of us are settled, have it made; others are restless, trying to make it. Some of us are happy people; others have forgotten how to laugh. Most of us are white; only a few, I'm afraid, are black or yellow or brown. Some of us have killed; others see death only on TV.

Some of us are awfully sure—about war's morality or immorality, about nuclear weapons and biological devastation, about American idealism or imperialism, about El Salvador and the Middle East; others are confused, uncertain, torn this way and that, even anxious about our own uncertainty. Some of us think your Church is "out of it," with no word of salvation for a world on the edge of damnation; others feel churchmen are saying too much. Some of us have stored up hate in our hearts; others agonize with love. Most of us are here because we still believe in you; some surely have come from curiosity, or protocol, or even despair.

Lord, we *are* a motley lot, aren't we?

196

II

Only one thing unites us at this moment, Lord: We all want peace. We are *all* convinced that war is hell. We *all* feel there is something tragically wrong when the governments of the world spend 450 billion dollars a year to kill, to threaten, to deter, to keep . . . peace. When millions of refugees water the roads with their tears. When babies are blasted to bits by bombs. When human beings are tortured beyond bearing by other "human" beings. We *all* weep for it, Lord—even those of us who feel that it cannot be otherwise, that it is not human but must be, that without war there will be no peace. Even those who are trained to kill and to destroy—surely most are nauseated at what they must do.

We all want life, Lord, and not death. We know the love and the anguish and the pain and the joy that conspire to create a single child. Many of us have shared with you the fashioning of human life. We sense how precious each life is to you, that to you too each of us is a sacred, irreplaceable I. And so we weep for each life that is snuffed out. We cannot rejoice when a headline proclaims that hundreds of the enemy have been slaughtered. For these are not statistics, Lord; these are persons. And when even one shrieks to heaven with his flesh in flames—friend or enemy—we all weep, we are all ashamed, we all want peace.

III

To our dismay, Lord, we have lost what we could not afford to lose: We have lost a peacemaker. He was not perfect, and his roots were in revolution. Repression was not foreign to him, and he died reviewing his weapons of war. But one shining day he left us breathless: He took one giant step towards peace. One day he dared the unthinkable: He flew unarmed into a city at war with him. One day he embraced an enemy he had vowed to destroy, sat next to a grand "old lady" and joked with joy. One day he touched our shores, and our hearts took wing: At a spot called "David" more fittingly than we knew, he signed "a framework for peace." One day he came to this capital, clasped hands with a president and a prime minister, pledged his country and his life to peace.

His life indeed; for now, Lord, the warmakers have killed him. And as we weep, part of his own world laughs in the streets: "We have destroyed the traitor." And so we weep all the more; for we much fear that "the impossible dream" is no longer possible. We wonder whether it was only a man who died, or if a world's hope died with him.

IV

But why, Lord, why? Must it always be so? We look back to a bloody balcony in Memphis, to a black preacher who had his own impassioned dream of peace. We look further back, to a hill outside Jerusalem, to a Jew who died half-naked and alone because, he said, we do not know the things that make for our peace. Your own Son, Lord! From Calvary to Cairo, must the prophets of peace be crucified for peace? Is this the price the peacemaker *must* be prepared to pay? Is it this you are trying to tell us from the shadows of the pyramids?

V

Which brings us back to ourselves, Lord, to our own hearts. For here is where peace and war are born. More radically than in the palaces of kings and the corridors of power. In *our* hearts.

If that is so, Lord, then who are we to cast stones at terrorists? We civilized folk across the world who kill more little innocents in a single year than we did in two world wars—because we are not quite sure they are human. We who let one fourth of humanity go to bed hungry each night—and announce the good news that their savior is free enterprise. We who mouth "Peace" to one another around an altar but will not forgive a hurt, a snub, a thoughtless insult, refuse to cross the desert of our pride. When did *I* last take a giant step, a small step, to a place of peace?

Today, Lord, we weep not so much for one fearless Egyptian; we weep for our fearful selves. For him we simply ask: Grant him, Lord, eternal peace. For ourselves: Change us, Lord; for we cannot change ourselves. If we are unshakable on the uses of war, keep us from being unloving. If we are uncertain on what makes for peace, let it not paralyze us. Take bitterness from us, even if we have cause to be bitter. Take hate from us, for we have never just cause for hatred. If we have bled, let the blood we shed be redemptive like your Son's. If we have grown fat over the flesh of others, scourge us till we cry out. Each of us knows what it is within us that makes for war. Prick our hearts with a sense of shame; for we have sinned, Lord, all of us—we have sinned against peace.

VI

We thank you, Lord, for one brave man, one bold peacemaker. In death we cannot let him die. Whoever we are, however we can, we take his burden on ourselves. We vow to move on, as he did, from wherever we have been; to renounce, as he did, our stubborn yesterdays; to dare, as he did, what we have never dared before; to take the first step, as he did, to an unthinkable future.

May this blessed peacemaker, this child of God, find peace at last. May he rest, Lord, in *your* peace.

Dahlgren Chapel
Georgetown University
October 16, 1981

EPILOGUE

34
LET IT HAPPEN TO ME
Fifty Years a Jesuit

- *Isaiah 66:10–14*
- *Philippians 1:3–11*
- *Luke 1:26–38, 46–55*

After fifty years, what does a Jesuit jubilarian preach? Not a string of academic credits, degrees earned and unearned. Not comical anecdotes or maudlin memories. Not an elegy over the sinking bark of Peter, a yearning for "the good old days." Not of such stuff are homilies fashioned. More pertinent are two probing questions: What does my Jesuit existence say to me? And, what Christian legacy can my experience leave to you?

My stimulus is the fair Lady whose song we celebrate in today's Gospel. Since some of you would be scandalized if my golden homily were not plated with three points, my reflections have for framework three facets of Mary's experience as recorded in Luke's opening chapter. First, Mary was "quite perplexed" (Lk 1:29). Second, Mary responded: "Let it happen to me according to your word" (1:38). Third, Mary sang: "My soul proclaims the greatness of the Lord" (1:46).

I

First, Mary was "quite perplexed." Perplexed indeed by the angel's greeting, "Hail, favored woman! The Lord is with you!" (Lk 1:28). But I think we can legitimately extend that. Perplexity, uncertainty, confusion would dot Mary's life from that moment on. When I was younger and more pious, I thought that Gabriel must have explained his message to Mary in great detail: how humanity

203

and divinity would be wed in her womb, why her Son would leave her, that he would be betrayed, die like a criminal on a cross—but not to worry, he will rise again! After all, if she was to mother God's Son, if she was to give God a human yes, she had to know what the contract called for, the bottom line.

I'm afraid it will not wash. Not so does Scripture speak of Mary—as of a woman with the future in the palm of her hand. Not such is our experience. Not mine, in any case. When I walked wide-eyed through the novitiate doors of St. Andrew-on-Hudson a half century ago, I had no God-given scenario for my life. Woodstock on the tawny Patapsco, Georgetown Hoyas and Saxas, *Theological Studies* and patristic theology, ecumunical council and ecumenical dialogue, even poverty, chastity, and obedience—these were not revealed by an angel. I did not know in detail what God was calling me to; I only knew, like Mary, that God was calling. As with Mary, He was letting me know only the first step, sketching only the broadest outline: for her, Mother of Jesus; for me, Society of Jesus. The story would be written as the years unfolded, as the world grew around me, as I grew. There would be confusion and questions, wonderment and uncertainty, changes and surprises, anger and fear and resentment, thorns and crosses. But at that first moment, when a novice we called "angel" welcomed me to a new life, there was nothing of this. The message from God was simple: Will you follow me in the Society of Jesus wherever I lead?

So too, I submit, for any Jesuit, for every Christian. When God asks "Will you?", He reveals very little: the basic call, the bare bones. His invitation does not include a vita, a biography, a script; and so it calls for an unbelievable faith, trust beyond imagining, your hand in God's. He does not promise a rose garden. He promises only that whatever the garden, Eden or Gethsemane, He will be there, faithful through all your infidelities. It's true of every vowed existence: husband and wife, priest or religious, the law or the dance, music or medicine, commerce or the Congress. It's true of the powerful and the powerless. God tells you only enough for you to say yes. Not a logical yes; rather the yes that was Mary's, the yes that shapes my second point.

II

Mary responded: "Let it happen to me according to your word" (Lk 1:38). Obviously and immediately, let that happen to me which you have spoken of: May I give birth through the Holy Spirit to him who will be called Son of God. But more is involved. With that response, Mary becomes the first Christian disciple. In fact, her life marks her as model of Christian discipleship. She lived what the Gospels proclaim: Doing the will of God is of greater value even than being mother of Jesus. It is Augustine's remarkable sentence: "Mary's relationship as mother would have been of no profit to her, had she not more joyfully borne Christ in her heart than in her body."[1] Time and again Luke gives us Mary as the woman who hears the word of God and keeps it, puts it into practice.[2] She hears that word not only from an angel; she hears it from the mouth of Jesus, hears it in the events of her life, from Nazareth to Calvary and beyond. And in each instance her response is the same fiat: "Let it happen to me according to your word."

That lesson in discipleship I find crucial to my Jesuit existence. The first fiat fifty years ago was easy enough. It was given in the flush of adolescence, when skin tone was glowing, energy was high octane, a strong right arm made for a fair shortstop, sauerkraut did not dictate diarrhea, and anxiety was a dictionary word. The world was my oyster. But "let it happen to me according to your word" is not a once-for-all affirmation. It grows more demanding with the years, when God's word is spoken through human events, by finite superiors, in harsh circumstances, when it is not so clear that it is God's word. Oh, it was distinctly God's word when it reflected my word: assigned early to the theology I loved; editing a powerful periodical; counseling popes and bishops; struggling for the unity of the churches; lecturing to perceptive people who "marveled at the words of grace" that fell from my lips (cf. Lk 4:22). Problems surge when what "happens" is unexpected or unwelcome or compels change from happy habits—when tragedy axes our roots. Some Jesuits have felt the agony in changes so drastic that they cry out: "This is not the Society I entered, not the Society in which I vowed obedience." I felt it when the Woodstock that housed my mind and heart for twenty-eight years was closed forever and, somewhat like Mary in the Temple, I "did not understand" what was being said to me (cf. Lk 2:50), could not hear the voice of God.

I dare not judge what others have done, their responses. I can only say what I see God trying to tell me through the thick fog of my human reasoning: Let go. Let go of yesterday. Yesterday is part of you, yes; you cannot forget it; but don't live in yesterday.

This, I suggest, is what Mary's life says to every Christian. To make "Let it happen to me" a living yes, you must let go of where you've been. Whether it's turning 21, 40, or 65; whether it's losing your health or your hair, your looks or your lustiness, your money or your memory, a person you love or a possession you prize—you have to move on. It's especially agonizing if you are tempted to cry: "This is not the Church I entered, not the Church to which I vowed fidelity." No jubilarian can program your response to change. I can only say: Essential to the Christian journey is a self-emptying more or less like Christ's; time and again, from womb to tomb, you have to let go. And to let go is to die a little. Not for its own sake, but because only by letting go, only by reaching out in trust into a shadowed future, can you come to be increasingly conformed to the dying-rising of Christ.

III

So then, on the one hand, perplexity, more than once; on the other hand, a ceaseless faith: God will do what He has promised; God will work His wonders in Mary as He sees fit to do. From such faith springs the song of Mary: "My soul proclaims the greatness of the Lord" (Lk 1:46). She is profoundly aware of the gulf that yawns between her "lowliness" and God's mightiness. Mary was not the mother of Jesus because she deserved to be; she gave birth to the Savior because "He who is mighty" did "great things" for her (1:49). *He* did it. God made her to mother in freedom the Savior of the world. And so her "spirit finds delight in God" (1:47). In God. She herself is delightful, and "all generations will count [her] blessed" (1:47); but only because God has "favored" her (1:28).

When I start thinking how fine a fellow I am, when I find myself staring, Narcissus-like, at the honorary degrees on my office wall, I recall a sobering incident. Over a decade ago, I was privileged to share an eightieth-birthday celebration for the distinguished British Jesuit Martin D'Arcy. An unusual group had been invited to a private dining room of the Club 21: the Duke and Duchess of Windsor, Paul Horgan, Phyllis McGinley, Senator and Mrs. Mansfield, and so on. In his response to the tribute I paid him, Father D'Arcy said very simply something I've never forgotten: "I suppose I've done some fairly good things in my lifetime.

But, you know, if God were not somehow there, it would all be rather silly, wouldn't it?"

Silly, indeed; in fact, impossible. In St. Augustine's powerful phrase, "If we but turn to God, that itself is a gift of God." Once I realize that, I can take a Christian delight in myself, in what a mighty God has done through a lowly man. I can like me!

And so for every Christian. There are two special sins that crucify Christ again: pride and despair. Each stems from the same heresy: The world can be saved by human wisdom. No, says St. Paul: "God chose what is low and despised in the world, even things that are not, to bring to nothing things that are, so that no human being might boast in the presence of God" (1 Cor 1:28–29). God chose you and me. Let God work His wonders in you, and you may take delight in God . . . and in yourself.

It is gloriously summed up in our Eucharist—a paean of praise and thanks: "Glory to God in the highest," "All glory and honor is yours, Almighty Father."

My brothers and sisters in Christ: What I should like to accent, to celebrate today is not myself, not some "great things" the Almighty has wrought through me. I want to celebrate the Society that has stimulated and supported me for half a century. I am not unaware of her human face. I would apply to the Society of Jesus what that fine French Jesuit Henri de Lubac once said about the Church of Christ:

> I am told that she is holy, yet I see her full of sinners. I am told that her mission is to tear man away from his earthy cares, to remind him of his eternal vocation, yet I see her constantly preoccupied with the things of the earth and of time, as if she wished us to live here forever. I am assured that she is universal, as open as divine intelligence and charity, and yet I notice very often that her members, through some sort of necessity, huddle together timidly in small groups—as human beings do everywhere. She is hailed as immutable, alone stable and above the whirlpools of history, and then, suddenly, under our very eyes, she upsets many of the faithful by the suddenness of her renewals.[3]

Yes, we are a society of sinners, even with the grace of God. Our vision is myopic, and so we do not always discern the divine, we misread the signs of the times. Our wills are weak, and so we do not always live the logic of our Jesuit commitment. Despite all our grandiose professions, we can be as small as the next man.

And still, here is where I want to be. In the midst of a world gone mad with passion and power, I find here a tradition of intelligence, of reason. Though occasionally dampened by the demands of obedience, I find here a freedom beyond compare, a freedom to grow, to become, yes to err. Despite the pettiness that can stalk unisex existence, I find here a community of openness, a community of love, a community that supports me without strangling me, a community on which I depend without being enslaved to it. In an age so grim and humorless, I share here rich joy and earthy laughter. And so I shall never cease to be grateful to my brothers in Christ, never cease saying to the Society of Jesus what the exiles in Babylon said to their own mother:

> If I forget you, O Jerusalem,
>   let my right hand wither!
> Let my tongue cleave to the roof of my mouth,
>   if I do not remember you,
> if I do not set Jerusalem
>   above my highest joy!
>
> (Ps 137:5–6)

My companions in Jesus, I thank you today for one gift above all others: Without you I could not murmur to God each day "Let it happen to me according to your word."

But this is not an in-house celebration, a Jesuit stag party. Today I celebrate all of you—and hundreds more who could not come. Why? Because each of you, without exception, has touched my life, enriched it. Because of you, I am different: more priestly, more Christian, more human. You have touched me in so many different ways, ways beyond counting. You have let me share your laughter and your tears, your head and your heart, your strength and your weakness. We have played and prayed, thought and fought, exchanged more bad jokes than good, have shared much of life and a small amount of death.

My deepest regret is that our very living keeps us apart. I see so rarely the smile in your eyes, rarely hear the music of your voice, rarely touch you in love. Fortunately, we have an eternity, endless days, to live and joy together. For, as I insist in one immortal line, if heaven is not for real, I shall be madder than hell. In the meantime, my feeling for you, and my prayer for you, is best expressed in the words you've heard from St. Paul's letter to the Christians at Philippi (Phil 1:3–11):

> I give thanks to my God each time I remember you. Always, in every prayer of mine for all of you, I make my prayer with joy, so full a part have you taken in the work of the gospel from the day it first reached you till now. Of this I am certain, that He who began the good work in you will bring it to completion, ready for the day when Jesus Christ comes. It is only fitting that I should feel this way about all of you: You are close to my heart, and I know that you share the same grace I do in defending and asserting the gospel. God is my witness, how I yearn for you all with the tenderness of Christ Jesus. And this is my prayer for you: May your love abound more and more, in the fulness of its knowledge and the depth of its perception, so that you may learn to prize what is of real value. May nothing cloud your conscience or hinder your progress till the day Christ comes. May you reap through Jesus Christ the full harvest of your justification to God's glory and praise.

To *God's* glory and praise. . . .

Dahlgren Chapel
Georgetown University
February 11, 14, and 15, 1981

NOTES

1. Antoine de Saint-Exupéry, *The Little Prince* (New York: Harcourt, Brace & World, c1943) 7–9.
2. See my *Tell the Next Generation: Homilies and Near Homilies* (New York: Paulist, c1980) 3–16, esp. 8–11.
3. Some works which may prove helpful: William F. Lynch, S.J., *Christ and Apollo: The Dimensions of the Literary Imagination* (New York: Sheed and Ward, c1960); Theodore W. Jennings, Jr., *Introduction to Theology: An Invitation to Reflection upon the Christian Mythos* (Philadelphia: Fortress, c1976) esp. 9–84; Amos Niven Wilder, *Theopoetic: Theology and the Religious Imagination* (Philadelphia: Fortress, c1976); Robert D. Young, *Religious Imagination: God's Gift to Prophets and Preachers* (Philadelphia: Westminster, c1979); Urban T. Holmes, III, *Ministry and Imagination* (New York: Seabury, c1976); Ray L. Hart, *Unfinished Man and the Imagination: Toward an Ontology and a Rhetoric of Revelation* (New York: Herder and Herder, 1968). Pertinent here, I suggest, is an understanding of symbol and of ritual; see, e.g., Mary Douglas, *Natural Symbols: Explorations in Cosmology* (New York: Penguin, 1978); George S. Worgul, *From Magic to Metaphor: A Validation of Christian Sacraments* (New York: Paulist, c1980).
4. I am aware that fantasy does not *have* to mean the bizarre; I am speaking of a common current usage. See *Webster's New International Dictionary of the English Language* (2nd ed. unabridged; Springfield, Mass.: Merriam, 1958) 918: "From the conception of *fantasy* as the faculty of mentally reproducing sensible objects, the meaning appears to have developed into: first, false or delusive mental creation; and second, any senselike representation in the mind, equivalent to the less strict use of *imagination* and *fancy*. Later *fantasy* acquired, also, a somewhat distinctive usage, taking over the sense of whimsical, grotesque, or bizarre image making. This latter sense, however, did not attach itself to the variant *phantasy*, which is used for visionary or phantasmic imagination." See also Holmes, *Ministry and Imagination* 100–103.
5. Holmes, *Ministry and Imagination* 97–98. Here Holmes is admittedly borrowing from Owen Barfield, *Saving the Appearances: A Study in Idolatry* (New York: Harcourt, Brace & World, n.d.).
6. Cf. Holmes 88.
7. Jennings, *Introduction to Theology* 49.
8. Cf. ibid. 52.

210

9. Sallie M. TeSelle, cited by Holmes, *Ministry and Imagination* 166, from the *Journal of the American Academy of Religion* 42 (1974) 635.
10. Jennings, *Introduction to Theology* 51.
11. Ibid. 51–52. See also Wilder, *Theopoetic* 80.
12. Avery Dulles, S.J., "The Symbolic Structure of Revelation," *Theological Studies* 41 (1980) 55–56.
13. Ibid. 56.
14. A. N. Whitehead, *The Aims of Education and Other Essays* (New York: Macmillan, 1929) 139.
15. Gerard Manley Hopkins, "As kingfishers catch fire . . . ," Poem 57 in W. H. Gardner and N. H. MacKenzie, eds., *The Poems of Gerard Manley Hopkins* (4th ed.; London: Oxford University, 1970) 90.
16. Wilder, *Theopoetic* 57.
17. Ibid. 67.
18. Vatican II, Constitution on the Sacred Liturgy, no. 35.
19. Frederick E. Flynn, in *Catholic Messenger* (Davenport, Iowa), Aug. 4, 1960, 13.
20. Holmes, *Ministry and Imagination* 221.
21. Here I am deeply indebted to Dulles, "The Symbolic Structure of Revelation" 55 ff. For objections raised against revelation as symbolic, and Dulles' reply, see ibid. 65–67.
22. Ibid. 59. The quotation from Perrin is taken from his *Jesus and the Language of the Kingdom* (Philadelphia: Fortress, 1976) 33.
23. See Dulles, ibid. 59–65.
24. Walter J. Burghardt, S.J., "From Classroom to Pulpit: How Preach Dogma?" *Proceedings of the Catholic Homiletic Society,* Fourth Annual Convention, Dec. 1961 (published at Kenrick Seminary, St. Louis) 23–35.
25. e. e. cummings, Poem 95 in *100 Poems.*
26. Nathan Mitchell, "Symbols Are Actions, Not Objects," *Living Worship* 13, no. 2 (Feb. 1977) 1–2.

Homily 1

1. The allusion is to a powerful contemporary film, *Ordinary People,* that reveals the destructive effects on a family when the father and mother live rather unthinkingly the kind of life their society expects of them.
2. *New York Times,* Nov. 28, 1980, B1.

Homily 2

1. For this second section, I have profited from the Introduction by John L. McKenzie, S.J., in his *Second Isaiah* (Anchor Bible 20; Garden City, N.Y.: Doubleday, 1968) esp. xv–xxx and xxxviii–lxvii.

2. I am using "Isaiah" as a convenient name for the different authors of what scholars call First Isaiah (chaps. 1–39), Second Isaiah (40–55), and Third Isaiah (56–66).

Homily 3

1. Schalom Ben-Chorin, as quoted by Hans Küng, *The Church* (New York: Sheed and Ward, 1968) 141.
2. Vatican II, Dogmatic Constitution on the Church, no. 5.
3. I am aware that many scholars prefer to translate "among you, in your midst" rather than "within you." But the point I am making is still valid: The kingship of Christ is mainly a matter of the interior man, the interior woman.
4. *Time*, Dec. 15, 1980, 74.

Homily 4

1. On the "seasons" see Daniel J. Levinson *et al., The Seasons of a Man's Life* (New York: Knopf, 1978).
2. Raymond E. Brown, S.S., "The Pater Noster as an Eschatological Prayer," *Theological Studies* 22 (1961) 190.
3. Vatican II, Constitution on the Church, no. 5. On the relationship between the Church of Christ and the kingdom of God, see John C. Haughey, S.J., "Church and Kingdom: Ecclesiology in the Light of Eschatology," *Theological Studies* 29 (1968) 72–86.
4. Cited from Norman Cousins, "The Promise of a University," *Scranton Journal* (University of Scranton) 1, no. 3 (Fall–Winter 1979) 6. This was originally an address delivered at the 1979 Annual Assembly of the Council for the Advancement and Support of Education; it was originally published in *CASE Currents.*
5. Reinhold Niebuhr, *The Irony of American History* (New York: Scribner's, 1952) 63.

Homily 5

1. Constitution on the Sacred Liturgy, no. 7.
2. Kotter and J. R. are references to characters in two contemporary TV series.
3. See Homily 32 below.

Homily 6

1. New York: Hawthorn, 1973.
2. For most of this first point, I am borrowing from my booklet *Towards*

Reconciliation (Washington, D.C.: United States Catholic Conference, 1974).

Homily 7

1. *Nestorii sermo* (Acta conciliorum oecumenicorum 1, 5, 1, 30); *Liber Heraclidis* (tr. F. Nau *et al.*, *Le Livre d'Héraclide de Damas* [Paris, 1910] 176); *Nestorii tractatus* (ACO 1, 5, 1, 38).
2. I am aware that some may challenge the bald statement "God died" as pastorally inappropriate, if not doctrinally debatable. I submit that the language of this paragraph is in harmony with a long-standing, defensible Catholic tradition, and that the brief explanation I give should keep a congregation from concluding that divinity, the divine nature, was destroyed. On this issue we are very much involved in the contemporary effort to rethink the mystery-laden "person" of Jesus.
3. Francis Thompson, "The Hound of Heaven," in Wilfred Meynell, ed., *Francis Thompson, Poems and Essays* (Westminster, Md.: Newman, 1949) 112.
4. William J. O'Malley, S.J., *The Voice of Blood* (Maryknoll, N.Y.: Orbis, 1980).

Homily 8

1. In the liturgy in Dahlgren Chapel that day we also celebrated the silver anniversary of Sister Mary K. Himens (campus minister at Georgetown University) in the Servants of the Holy Heart of Mary.
2. For the understanding of this difficult passage, I am much indebted to Raymond E. Brown, S.S., *The Gospel according to John (xiii–xxi)* (Anchor Bible 29A; Garden City, N.Y.: Doubleday, 1970) 1101–22.
3. In this section on the prediction and fact of Peter's denial, I am combining the four Gospel accounts, despite my awareness that not all the details given by the individual Evangelists can be harmonized. Cf. Lk 22:31–34, 54–62; Mk 14:26–31, 66–72; Mt 26:30–35, 69–75; Jn 13:36–38 and 18:15–18, 25–27. We are most likely dealing with varying forms of a common tradition; see Brown (n. 2 above) 616.
4. Brown, ibid. 838–39, has a useful comparative chart of Peter's three denials.
5. For this interpretation see the discussion in Brown, ibid. 1106–8, 1117–22.
6. In this paragraph I am adapting portions of a remarkable conference by John Courtney Murray, S.J., "The Danger of the Vows," *Woodstock Letters* 96 (1967) 421–27. For a similar but more extended use of the same ideas, see my *Tell the Next Generation: Homilies and Near Homilies* (New York: Paulist, 1980) 87–89.

7. Gerard Manley Hopkins, "God's Grandeur," in W. H. Gardner and N. H. MacKenzie, eds., *The Poems of Gerard Manley Hopkins* (4th ed.; New York: Oxford University, 1970) 66.
8. For an informative presentation of Mary Magdalene as "the apostle to the apostles," see Raymond E. Brown, S.S., "Roles of Women in the Fourth Gospel," in Walter J. Burghardt, ed., *Woman: New Dimensions* (New York: Paulist, c1977) 112–23, at 116 ff. This article appeared earlier in *Theological Studies* 36 (1975) 688–99; see specifically 692 ff.

Homily 9

1. Norman Cousins, *Anatomy of an Illness as Perceived by the Patient: Reflections on Healing and Regeneration* (New York: Bantam Books, 1981) 72–73.
2. Borrowed from a short poem by Sister Mary Ignatius, "Discovery," in *Messenger of the Sacred Heart* 77, no. 2 (February 1942) 58.
3. This second point owes much to a small section on "life" in Raymond E. Brown, S.S., *The Gospel according to John (i–xii)* (Garden City, N.Y.: Doubleday, 1966) 505–8.

Homily 10

1. See William F. Arndt and F. Wilbur Gingrich, *A Greek-English Lexicon of the New Testament and Other Early Christian Literature* (Chicago: University of Chicago, 1957) 505. The Greek expression *menein en* occurs ten times in verses 4–10 of chapter 15.
2. St. Augustine, *On Holy Virginity* 3 (PL 40, 398); *Sermon 215*, no. 4 (PL 38, 1074).
3. See Karl Stern, *The Flight from Woman* (New York: Farrar, Straus, and Giroux, 1965) 9–57, especially 18 and 53–54.
4. Ibid. 19.
5. See, e.g., Raymond E. Brown, S.S., *The Gospel according to John (xiii–xxi)* (Garden City, N.Y.: Doubleday, 1970) 672–74.
6. Ibid. 674.

Homily 11

1. T. S. Eliot, *Murder in the Cathedral* (New York: Harcourt, Brace, c1935) 48.
2. For much useful information on the biblical notions of peace, I am indebted to Xavier Léon-Dufour, "Peace," in his *Dictionary of Biblical Theology* (2nd ed.; New York: Seabury, 1973) 411–14, and John L. McKenzie, S.J., "Peace," in his *Dictionary of the Bible* (New York: Macmillan, c1965) 651–52.

3. From a poem by Sister Mary Ignatius, "Discovery," *Messenger of the Sacred Heart* 77, no. 2 (February 1942) 58.

Homily 12

1. Leo the Great, *First Sermon for Christmas* 3 (Sources chrétiennes 22bis, 72).
2. A startling statement on the face of it, but a favorite refrain of the Fathers of the Church, especially the Eastern writers.

Homily 13

1. In Wilfrid Ward, *The Life of John Henry Cardinal Newman* 2 (New York: Longmans, Green, 1912) 147.
2. See William F. Orr and James Arthur Walther, *I Corinthians* (Anchor Bible 32; Garden City, N.Y.: Doubleday, 1976) 279–83. On the eight New Testament lists of charisms, see W. F. Dicharry, "Charism: In the Bible," *New Catholic Encyclopedia* 3 (1967) 460.
3. The reference is to a contemporary sport: appraising human beauty, male or female attractiveness, on a scale from one to ten. As I write, there is a popular movie entitled "10."
4. I am aware that the Greek simply reads "for the advantage," without specifying whose advantage; but the context (vv. 8–10) seems to make it clear that the gifts are intended for the general good.

Homily 14

1. See Carroll Stuhlmueller, C.P., in *Jerome Biblical Commentary* (Englewood Cliffs, N.J.: Prentice-Hall, 1968) 44:69.
2. See Jacques Dupont, *Les Béatitudes* 1: *Le problème littéraire—Les deux versions du Sermon sur la montagne et des Béatitudes* (new ed.; Louvain: Nauwelaerts, 1958) 209–23.
3. For the following see Dupont, *Les Béatitudes* 2: *La bonne nouvelle* (new ed.; Paris: Gabalda, 1969) 13–51.
4. For the following see Dupont, ibid. 2, 53–90.
5. Ibid. 2, 380.
6. From a perceptive brief commentary on the liturgical readings for the Sixth Sunday of the Year by Joseph A. Tetlow, S.J., "A Prickly Pair," *America* 142, no. 5 (Feb. 9, 1980) iii.

Homily 15

1. Rosemary Haughton, "In Exchange with God," *National Catholic Reporter* 15, no. 32 (June 1, 1979) 1 and 8.

Homily 16

1. Within this paragraph I have profited from Joachim Jeremias, *The Parables of Jesus* (rev. ed.; New York: Scribner's, c1963) 202–5.

Homily 17

1. Alexander Pope, *An Essay on Criticism,* line 525.
2. Dan Otto Via, Jr., *The Parables: Their Literary and Existential Dimension* (Philadelphia: Fortress, c1967) 139.
3. Francis Thompson, "The Hound of Heaven," in Wilfred Meynell, ed., *Francis Thompson, Poems and Essays* (Westminster, Md.: Newman, 1949) 112.

Homily 18

1. I put the matter this way because some scholars are convinced that Jesus did not understand himself as the Servant of the Lord, much less as the suffering atoning servant of Isa 53, while they are ready to recognize that "this interpretation did come into the Palestinian church very early" (thus Reginald H. Fuller, *The Foundations of New Testament Christology* [New York: Scribner's, c1965] 118–19). For the conviction that Jesus did see his mission in the light of Isa 53:1–2, see Joseph Coppens, *Le messianisme et sa relève prophétique* (Gembloux: Duculot, 1974) 181–216.
2. A homily is not the place to discuss the disputed question whether or to what extent Paul was responsible for the hymn in Phil 2:6–11.
3. Translation from Joseph A. Fitzmyer, in *Jerome Biblical Commentary* (Englewood Cliffs, N.J.: Prentice-Hall, 1968) 2:250.
4. On this text, the only logion where Jesus cites a passage certainly taken from the fourth Servant Song, see Coppens, *Le messianisme* 209.
5. Thomas Merton, *Conjectures of a Guilty Bystander* (Garden City, N.Y.: Doubleday Image Books, 1956) 261.

Homily 19

1. See, e.g., Joachim Jeremias, *The Parables of Jesus* (rev. ed.; New York: Scribner's, c1963) 65. I am indebted to Jeremias for a number of pertinent insights into these parables; see ibid. 63–69, 176–80, 187–90.
2. See the splendidly informative article by Eugene A. LaVerdière, S.S.S., and William G. Thompson, S.J., "New Testament Communities in Transition: A Study in Matthew and Luke," *Theological Studies* 37 (1976) 567-97.

3. See Homily 2 for much the same problem of Catholic identity, with greater stress on the difficulty in spelling it out.

Homily 20

1. For this first point, I have profited from the articles on "Glory," "Praise," and "Thanksgiving" in Xavier Léon-Dufour, ed., *Dictionary of Biblical Theology* (2nd ed.; New York: Seabury, 1973) 202-5, 442-45, 598-600.
2. Thomas Merton, *Conjectures of a Guilty Bystander* (Garden City: Doubleday, 1966) 140-41.
3. John Donne, *Holy Sonnets,* no. 15.

Homily 21

1. Christopher Dickey and Samuel Allis, in the *Washington Post,* Oct. 4, 1979, A17.
2. Ibid. A1.
3. *Time,* Oct. 15, 1979, 44.
4. James Reston, quoted in *Time,* ibid. 40.

Homily 22

1. See Homily 33 in this volume.
2. Dan Otto Via, Jr., *The Parables: Their Literary and Existential Dimension* (Philadelphia: Fortress, c1967) 118–19.
3. Cf. ibid. 119.

Homily 23

1. Cf. B. J. Alfrink, "L'Idée de résurrection d'après Dan., XII, 1–2," *Biblica* 40 (1959) 355–71.
2. So Louis F. Hartman, C.SS.R., "Daniel," *Jerome Biblical Commentary* (Englewood Cliffs, N.J.: Prentice-Hall, c1968) 26:34.
3. "Current Comment," *America* 141, no. 15 (Nov. 17, 1979) 290.
4. *Time* 114, no. 20 (Nov. 12, 1979) 42.

Homily 24

1. I have developed this point at greater length in a much earlier homily, "The Trinity: Mystery of Love," published in my collection *All Lost in Wonder: Sermons on Theology and Life* (Westminster, Md.: Newman, 1960) 3-8.

2. Phyllis McGinley, "In Praise of Diversity," in *The Love Letters of Phyllis McGinley* (New York: Viking, 1954) 12–16.
3. Only the pedant would complain that orthodoxy calls for distinct, not "separate," Persons. Anyhow, "distinct" would destroy the meter.

Homily 25

1. This translation of part of the "Fifth Lecture on the Mysteries" (nos. 20–22) is borrowed almost totally from Anthony A. Stephenson's version in *The Works of Saint Cyril of Jerusalem* 2 (Fathers of the Church 64; Washington, D.C.: Catholic University of America, c1970) 202–3. Scholars are at odds on the author and date of the five mystagogical catecheses. Is the author Cyril of Jerusalem (bishop 348–86) or John II of Jerusalem (bishop 387–417) or a combination of both? For a summary discussion of the issues, see ibid. 143–51.
2. Gerard Manley Hopkins, "S. Thomae Aquinatis Rhythmus ad SS. Sacramentum 'Adoro te supplex, latens deitas,' " in W. H. Gardner and N. H. MacKenzie, eds., *The Poems of Gerard Manley Hopkins* (4th ed.; New York: Oxford University, 1970) 211.
3. "Fourth Lecture on the Mysteries," no. 1 (tr. Stephenson, FC 64, 181).
4. For a treatment of this idea in patristic literature, see my essay "The Body of Christ: Patristic Insights," in K. E. Skydsgaard *et al.*, *The Church as the Body of Christ* (Notre Dame, Ind.: University of Notre Dame, 1963) 69–101.

Homily 26

1. This paragraph has profited from a conference by the General of the Society of Jesus, Pedro Arrupe, "The Trinitarian Inspiration of the Ignatian Charism" (nos. 18–22), given at the closing session of the Ignatian Course, Feb. 8, 1980, at the Ignatian Spirituality Center in Rome, and reproduced for private circulation by the Maryland Province of the Society of Jesus.
2. From a remarkable essay by Karl Rahner, S.J., in *Ignatius of Loyola* (New York: Collins, 1979) 12.
3. See Hugo Rahner, S.J., *Ignatius the Theologian* (New York: Herder and Herder, 1968) 58.
4. For interesting material on the devotion of Ignatius of Loyola to Ignatius of Antioch, see James Brodrick, S.J., *Saint Ignatius Loyola: The Pilgrim Years* (London: Burns & Oates, 1956) 284–87.
5. To grasp the concerns of this homily, one should realize that it was delivered to Jesuits only—specifically, Jesuits of the District of Columbia and its environs.

Homily 27

1. For the Pauline ideas in this section and the next, I have been helped much by the slim, rich work of Joseph A. Fitzmyer, S.J., *Pauline Theology: A Brief Sketch* (Englewood Cliffs, N.J.: Prentice-Hall, c1967), especially 63–73.
2. Cyril of Jerusalem, *Mystagogical Lectures* 2, 4–5. I have reproduced the translation by Anthony A. Stephenson in the series The Fathers of the Church 64 (Washington, D.C.: Catholic University of America, c1970). 163–65. On the author of the catechetical lectures, see note 1 to my Homily 25 above.

Homily 28

1. I have profited from the informative article by François Amiot, "Temple," in Xavier Léon-Dufour, *Dictionary of Biblical Theology* (2nd ed.; New York: Seabury, 1973) 594–97.

Homily 29

1. These last four sentences owe a debt to Pierre Fransen, "Towards a Psychology of Divine Grace," *Cross Currents* 8 (1958) 229–30.
2. Quoted in *Time*, Dec. 29, 1975, 48.
3. For the record, it may be pointed out that this homily was offered at a liturgy during the Pre-Study Day for Bishops, Priests, and Deacons, held in conjunction with the Third Annual National Catholic Lay Celebration of Evangelization.

Homily 30

1. John C. Haughey, *Should Anyone Say Forever?* (Image Books; Garden City, New York: Doubleday, 1977). This is a remarkably insightful, provocative book. The distinguished anthropologist Margaret Mead often turned to it in the last months of her life.
2. Quoted in *Time*, Sept. 14, 1970, 34.

Homily 31

1. e. e. cummings, Poem 95 in *100 Poems*.

Homily 34

1. Augustine, *On Holy Virginity* 3.

2. See, on this point, the informative, inspiring article by Patrick J. Bears-ley, S.M., "Mary the Perfect Disciple: A Paradigm for Mariology," *Theological Studies* 41 (1980) 461–504.

3. Henri de Lubac, S.J., "Meditation on the Church," in John H. Miller, C.S.C., ed., *Vatican II: An Interfaith Appraisal* (Notre Dame: University of Notre Dame, c1966) 259.